The ROLLING STONES

TONY JASPER

CONTENTS

First published 1976 by Octopus Books Limited
59 Grosvenor Street, London W.1.

© 1976 Octopus Books Limited

ISBN 0 7064 0549 8

Produced by Mandarin Publishers Limited
22a Westlands Road, Quarry Bay, Hong Kong
Printed in Hong Kong

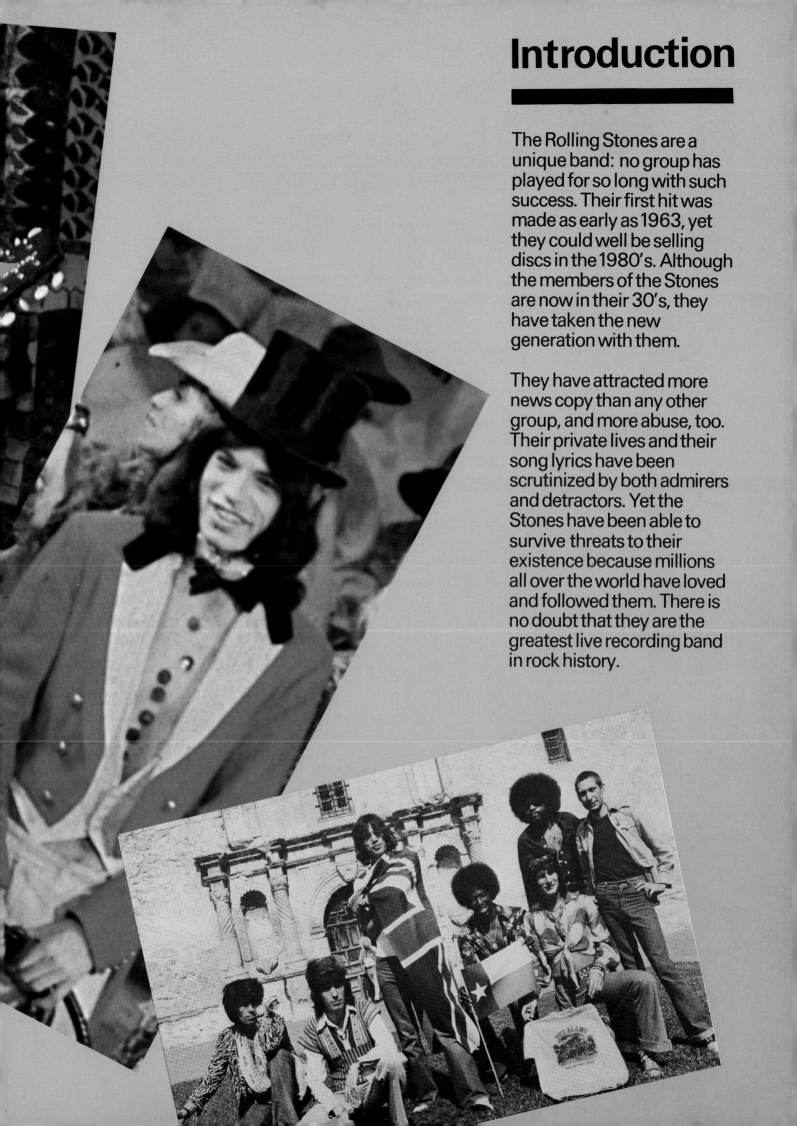

Introduction

The Rolling Stones are a unique band: no group has played for so long with such success. Their first hit was made as early as 1963, yet they could well be selling discs in the 1980's. Although the members of the Stones are now in their 30's, they have taken the new generation with them.

They have attracted more news copy than any other group, and more abuse, too. Their private lives and their song lyrics have been scrutinized by both admirers and detractors. Yet the Stones have been able to survive threats to their existence because millions all over the world have loved and followed them. There is no doubt that they are the greatest live recording band in rock history.

THEIR STORY

The music critics and fans were disappointed with the first Rolling Stones single, 'Come On'. The song's source was a Chuck Berry album, appropriately titled, with singular lack of imagination, *Chuck Berry*, a disc which had hovered for some weeks in the lower end of the Top Twenty album listings.

'Come On' by the Rolling Stones did not represent the kind of mood and style typified by the five when they played at their resident club, the Station Hotel, Richmond, Surrey. Even group member, harmonica-playing Brian Jones felt slightly awkward with the group's choice of song and performance. He said, 'Once we've made an impression, then we can try out our real rhythm and blues routines.'

At Richmond they sang and played less commercial Berry, numbers like 'Bye Bye Johnny' and 'Down The Road Apiece', and gave their interpretation of Chuck Berry's treatment of Nat King Cole's 'Route 66'. They also featured Bo Diddley songs.

People were queuing long before opening-time—the group had become popular after only a few appearances. Previous to appearing at Richmond the group, Mick Jagger, Brian Jones, Bill Wyman, Keith Richard, Charlie Watts, and for a time, pianist and organist, Ian Stewart, had spent afternoons rehearsing at the Wetherby Arms, in Chelsea and, in the evenings, gigging at the Ealing Jazz Club, the Marquee Jazz Club, the Red Lion and the Flamingo club, London.

It was Brian Jones who heard that the Dave Wood Rhythm-and-Blues Band were leaving the Station hotel. Mick Jagger telephoned the club owner, Giorgio Gomelsky to discover that the latter had been about to phone him with an offer of playing at the Richmond club.

Individually, Stone members had played with an assortment of bands and groups with a non-musical setting providing the initial base of the group, when Brian Jones by chance found himself in Mick Jagger and Keith Richard's favourite drinking haunt. Later the three with their common music love shared a flat plus a Muddy Waters album, and on this disc was a track called 'Rolling Stones'. It seemed an ideal name for their projected group and dreams of bigtime.

'Come On' was issued in June 1963, a few months after the group had become the centre of press attention. The earliest record paper interest came from *Record Mirror* and their features editor, Peter Jones. He commissioned writer Norman Jopling and photographer Bill Williams to provide copy and pictures on the group.

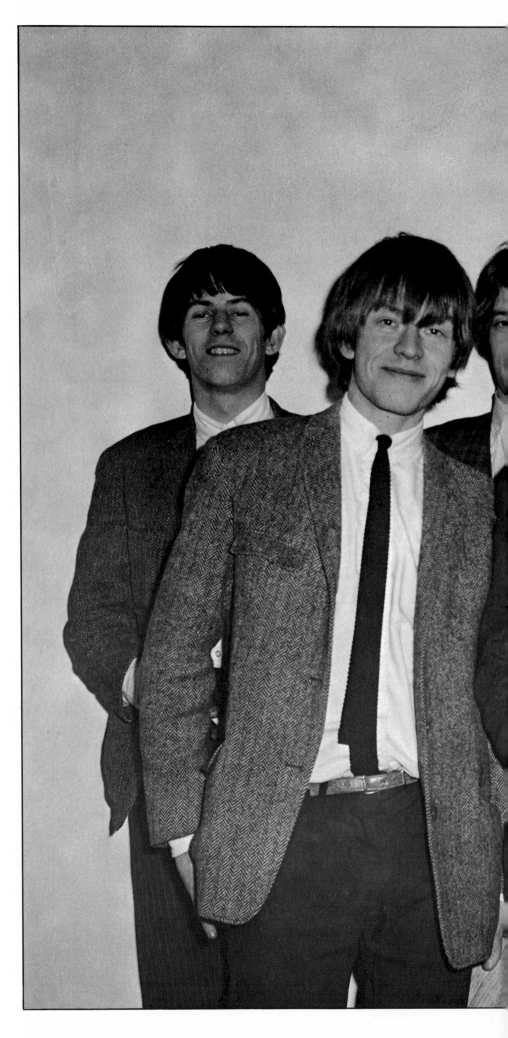

Peter Jones also informed a young publicist, Andrew 'Loog' Oldham, of the group's potential both as musicians and as future stars. Oldham's interest was immediate and together with show-business agent, Eric Easton, he went to hear the Stones at their Richmond venue. The outcome was the duo becoming the Stones' managers with an agreement that they should be in charge of the group's recording sessions. For this a separate company called Impact Sound was formed.

Decca signed up the Stones, doubtless smarting from their turning-down of the Beatles and desperate for another group with similar commercial potential. By the early summer the Beatles had made Number Two with 'Please Please Me' and topped the charts with 'From Me to you'. August brought a further top spot with 'She Loves You'.

The recording sessions for their first single from the Stones had been far from happy occasions with numerous re-takes, since it was felt that the club sound was not being reproduced in the studio setting.

However, 'Come On' was issued. Interestingly, though, Decca did not include the single in its full-page advertisement in *Record Mirror* of 8 June, 1963, but gave it space in the less lavish quarters of page six with an advertisement only $1\frac{1}{2}$ by $2\frac{1}{4}$ inches— a far cry from later single-, double-page and more generally four- and eight-page supplements of advertising.

Left: The group, early and unsophisticated. Below: Performing for an audience of 16,000 at Longleat, 1964.

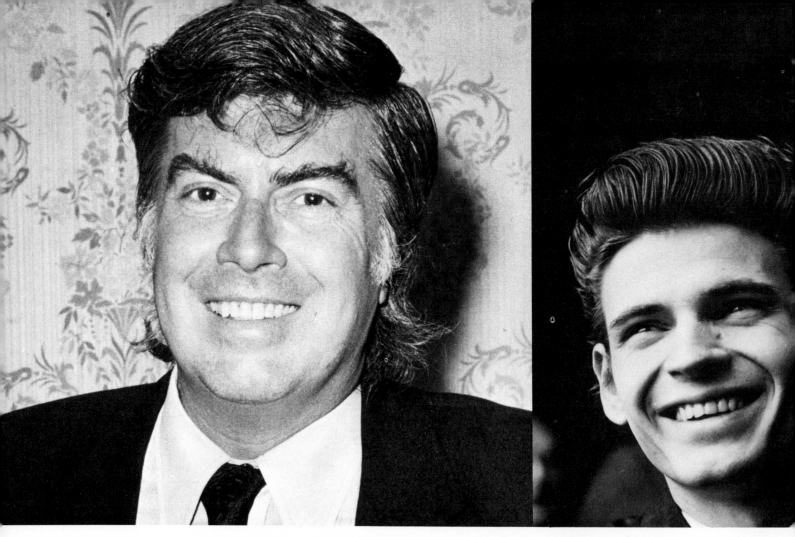

The single took time before making its first entry on 27 July at 50, the lowest chart position, which in sales terms meant a weekly sale of only a few hundred copies. It proceeded on a chart path of 32, 28, 25, 24, 23, 24, 22, 21, 22, 26, 29, 42 and alas, no more. While it made its chart entry, the more successful discs around at the time were in the US, Jan & Dean's 'Surf City', the Tymes' 'So Much in Love', and 'Easier Said Than Done' by David Essex; in the UK Australian Frank Ifield topped the charts with 'Confessin''. He was followed by 'Devil in Disguise' from Elvis Presley and the Liverpool group, The Searchers, with 'Sweets For My Sweet'.

On the strength of a moderate chart entry, general chat in daily and music papers, and their sensed potential, the Stones began their first British tour on 29 September. The 30-date tour saw the group on the same billing as their hero, Bo Diddley, and the admired Everly Brothers. For the Stones, the first tour was obviously a basic experience of coping with travel demands and continually meeting new audiences, a somewhat different situation from playing in front of a regular 'home' crowd.

They were relatively raw. They were very keen to see their ambitions and dreams being realized but were to some degree unaware of their public image and what the media might build up and invent around them.

Keith Richard saw the tour as an opportunity of picking the guitar brains of Everly Brothers guitarist, Don Peake. Bill Wyman had noticed the beginning of fan hysteria when their fans began paying them undue personal attention and removing letters and numbers from their car registration plates. He also noticed the ecstatic home reception given to Brian Jones when the Stones played at Cheltenham. Brian was known as 'our local lad with yellow hair'.

Brian was thrilled at playing on the same bill as the 'hip-king of R & B', Bo Diddley, while Jagger was excited by the late addition of Little Richard on their tour. He also seemed slightly put out by frequent smashing of dressing-room windows by fans who threw a flurry of 'autograph books, stones, sweets and cigarettes'.

The follow-up single came near the tour's end. At one stage it was to have been 'Fortune Seller', a song from an American blues album of the time, We Sing The Blues, a collection of cuts from the Benny Spellman catalogue. However, the released disc was a Beatle song penned for the group, 'I Wanna Be Your Man' and a recording stemming from the same occasion as 'Come On' on the B side.

Ian Stewart played piano on 'I Wanna Be Your Man'. He was now the group's road manager. Release date was 1 November, two weeks before release of the album, With The

Beatles, a disc with the then highest ever advance order for an LP of 250,000 copies.

'I Wanna Be Your Man' made the Top Twenty and was the last disc for many, many years not to make the Top Ten and indeed, apart from 'We Love You' coupled with 'Dandelion', the Top Five.

The disc entered the Record Mirror Top Fifty on 16 November at 41. The following week it was 32, then 30, 16, 15, 13, 14, 15, 12, 14, 15, 17 and on 8 February the disc passed out of the Top Twenty to position 24. The length of stay, the fact of the second single having reached Number Twelve had set the seal on the future Stones' success, though perhaps only the far-seeing could visualize the group becoming the centre of the nation's adult consideration during the lateish '60s in Britain.

By September 1964, less than twelve months after the group's first ever tour and Top Twenty single, momentous changes had occurred. They had reached their fourth tour of Britain and were now topping the bill ahead of people like Charlie and Inez Fox, The Mojos and Mike Berry. Europe had tasted their musical wares and the group had made frequent appearances on British television. Their discs sold well. An EP which sold for almost twice the price of a single nevertheless made some singles listings and in the EP charts it was so

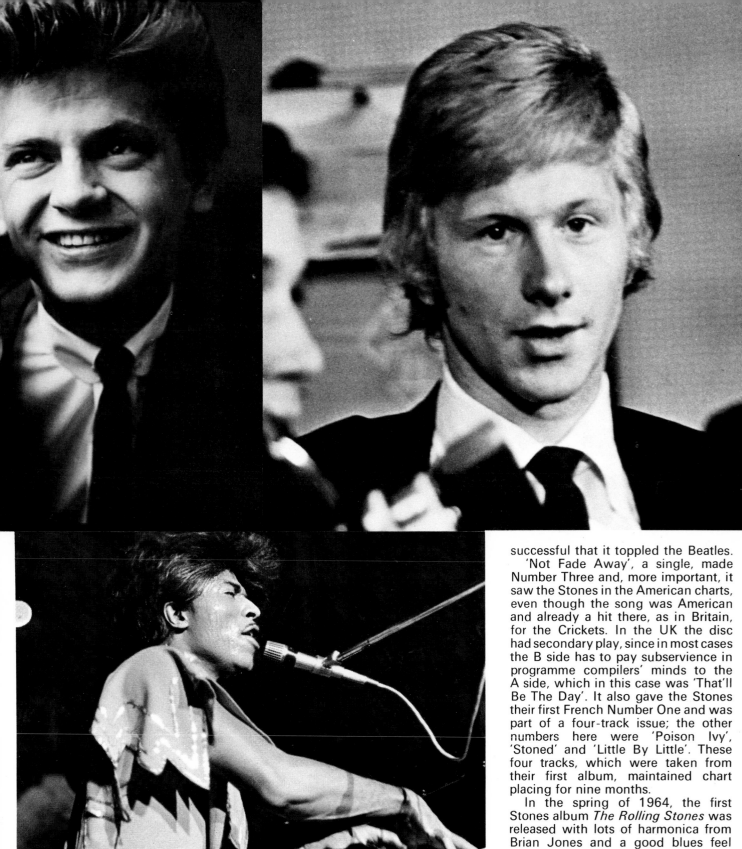

successful that it toppled the Beatles.

'Not Fade Away', a single, made Number Three and, more important, it saw the Stones in the American charts, even though the song was American and already a hit there, as in Britain, for the Crickets. In the UK the disc had secondary play, since in most cases the B side has to pay subservience in programme compilers' minds to the A side, which in this case was 'That'll Be The Day'. It also gave the Stones their first French Number One and was part of a four-track issue; the other numbers here were 'Poison Ivy', 'Stoned' and 'Little By Little'. These four tracks, which were taken from their first album, maintained chart placing for nine months.

In the spring of 1964, the first Stones album *The Rolling Stones* was released with lots of harmonica from Brian Jones and a good blues feel pervading its content. There was even a tribute to legendary producer Phil Spector in an instrumental, 'Now I've Got A Witness', which was sub-titled 'Like Uncle Phil and Uncle Gene'. Spector had been at the London Regent Sound studio session for 'Not Fade Away', and with Mick Jagger had written the B side number 'Little By Little'.

During the short time between the first and fourth British tour they had met Gene Pitney at a recording for the Independent Television pop show Thank Your Lucky Stars. Keith Richard

Top left: Peter Jones, the first influential figure to sense the Stones' potential. Top centre: The Everlys – hit American duo billed with the Stones on their first U.K. tour.

Top right: Andrew Loog Oldham, who was the first manager of the group. Above: Little Richard, who was a late addition to the artist roster of the first tour.

and Mick Jagger were certain they had a hit for Pitney with a song called 'That Girl Belongs To Yesterday'. Pitney recorded the song and it became a big hit both sides of the Atlantic. It also showed first signs of the prolific Jagger—Richard song-writing partnership.

The Stones album shot straight up the charts and made Number One. In America an exerpt from the album, 'Tell Me', was issued as a single and made the Top Thirty.

And so it was that, less than nine months after that first UK tour, the Stones headed for the States and into the world of cheering fans at the airport, interviews and photo calls, a meeting with famed DJ, Murray K, and hotel captivity. Fans surrounded the building and the police wanted the group inside; in this historical context, at least it was a hotel! They visited numerous major American cities and, doubtless with due respect to the programme's rating, appeared on the Hollywood Palace Television show in Los Angeles. If the British pop paper *Record Mirror* had called the group 'the hirsute quintet' as a change from the more common, 'long-haired five', then the programme's compere, Dean Martin, seemed less polite. Martin had quips like 'Their hair is not that long. It's just smaller foreheads and higher eyebrows.'

The Stones were part of a larger package than was customary at the time for British tours. With them were Bobby Vee, The Chiffons, Bobby Comstock and Bobby Goldsboro. It was not an unsuccessful visit, merely low-key in terms of future reaction.

Whilst in the States they recorded at the Chess Record Company headquarters studio in Chicago and as they toured America, so they learnt of their British chart triumphs and poll awards. In the *Record Mirror* Pop Poll (votes added up from readers' listings) they came second in the 'World Section—Male Vocal Group' behind the Beatles. Surprisingly, they only managed fourth position in the instrumental ratings, though possibly readers may not have considered them as instrumentalists in view of the vocals in their music. However, in the British section they went ahead of the Beatles, taking first place, and Mick Jagger easily beat Hank B. Marvin of The Shadows in the 'Individual Group Member' section. 'Not Fade Away' came second in the category 'Best Disc of 1963 and 1964'. The results were published in *Record Mirror's* Tenth Anniversary edition on 20 June 1964.

Andrew Oldham ceased to be the Stones' manager at the end of summer

The five rehearse for the British T.V. programme, Thank Your Lucky Stars.

1964, though he retained interests in recording the Stones. He had also found an incredibly beautiful girl called Marianne Faithfull, given her a Jagger–Richard composition, 'As Tears Go By', and scored a Top Ten hit.

By the end of 1964 the Stones had been voted number one in the *Melody Maker* Pop Poll's Vocal Instrumental Group and possessed the year's best single, 'Not Fade Away'.

The single reflected the Stones of 1963–4 and for some young people caught up with speed, it was a useful aid. By July 1965 the game had changed. The Stones' lyrics had come to be seen as impudent challenges to society's practices and niceties (though perhaps the two words are synonymous here).

A succession of singles roared up the charts, ones called 'Satisfaction', '19th Nervous Breakdown', 'Have You Seen Your Mother, Baby?' and the disc tailor-made for loud parties, 'Get Off Of My Cloud'.

Mick Jagger had become more given to inflammatory statements or perhaps he was tired of often insolent media employees and an amazingly twisted adult public which saw him and the Stones as a divisive influence on parent–child relationships. By drawing attention to this they merely added 'fuel to the fire' with their emotive pronouncements on the Stones, their hair, supposed life-style, music and 'general' ethos.

Amidst the record and tour successes the Stones, or at least a few of them, had taken the first steps towards affluent living. Charlie Watts bought himself a splendid sixteenth-century house; he and the others may have had some inner yearnings for a respectable British life-style but there were very radical discrepancies between their thoughts and actions and the upright image.

Doubtless British aristocrats and lordly figures have indulged in somewhat unseemly acts but such adventures usually remain hidden or referred to as 'high jinks'. For the Stones, however, public life became a series of widely reported activities. Mid-1965 saw Bill Wyman, Mick Jagger and Brian Jones in court for urinating in the forecourt of a filling station. It became breakfast-time reading for the British nation.

The Stones were now public, they were life-style actors calling forth extremes of passion, they were either hated or loved. Most of those who felt less strongly followed the Beatles instead. The Liverpool four were awarded honours, they were made Members of the British Empire. And at a time when it mattered whether one wore a tie or jacket to enter most hotels and restaurants, the Beatles complied, whilst the Stones did not. The latter were ahead of their time.

America had seen the group on the famous Ed Sullivan show and amidst its dire conservatism, the Stones seemed monsters from another planet or urchins surviving from nineteenth-century Britain. Mid '66 saw the Stones suing fourteen American hotels who had refused the group right to stay, and while the battle raged, their records sold in millions, and for thousands of young people across both sides of the Atlantic and much of the English-speaking world, the Stones were 'kings'.

After their August concert at London's Royal Albert Hall, the Stones, at an after-performance party, received 22 gold discs, one for each of their records with one million sales.

Thus their British tour began with a flourish, though the Albert Hall audience had made their mark with hundreds of fans racing towards the stage as soon as the house lights dimmed. Order was only restored under threat of abandoning the concert.

Riots for the Stones had become quite normal throughout countless countries. The only difference between, for example, the Stones in Britain and say, in Sweden, came from some changes in the Stones' record releases and successes. While 'She Said Yeah' from the album *Out Of Our Heads* was a smash in Sweden 'Fortune Teller' was Number One in Australia.

In spite of overwhelming success and adulation from countless fans, the Stones were not without their critics. A letter in *Record Mirror* (7 January 1967) from Phil Luce of St Ouen, Jersey in the Channel Islands said:

Look at all the mistakes which they [the Stones] have made this year. There was that stupid photograph of the Stones dressed as women. Their clothes don't suit them like they used to. Their hair has changed for the worse. They have become lazy. They don't try as hard as they used to with their recordings. . . . The Stones are still the greatest but are capable of much better things.

There was indeed truth in what he said but then some of the Stones were having personal problems, like Mick Jagger with his three-year-old rela-

Top: Keith, Brian, Mick and excited audience. Middle: Mick with Marianne Faithfull. Bottom: With producer, Phil Spector. Right: Closeups of all of the members of the Rolling Stones, during a recording of the T.V. show Thank Your Lucky Stars. The Stones always had at least two 'house' photographers and are probably the most photographed group of all time. Overleaf: The Stones in full steam at London's Wembley Stadium, May 1968.

tionship with Chrissie Shrimpton. It ended and thus snapped a link for Mick with 'unknown' and comparatively penniless days, for the two had been together almost from the beginning of the group's recording career. Marianne Faithfull was now his girlfriend.

And Jagger more than the other members, with the exception of Brian Jones, had problems with being a star and with his own identity. Months previously he had collapsed in New York. He had been driving himself hard with recordings and rehearsals for the ensuing American tour. Also he had begun taking acid and obviously saw no danger in this, in spite of seeing the gradual disintegration of Brian Jones which was partly caused by LSD and other mind-expanding drugs.

In 1967 there were several Rolling Stones sensations within a few months. The first came with the 21 January new entry single, 'Let's Spend The Night Together'. The British press waxed hot, as did countless popular figures given to public statements. The Stones were evidently suggesting copulation.

The controversy was avoided in the States where the disc's B side, 'Ruby Tuesday', became the hit, and when the group sang the song on the Ed Sullivan show its title had become 'Let's Spend Some Time Together'. Strangely enough, the Stones felt 'Ruby Tuesday' was the better track of the two in terms of musical achievement and successful recording.

While the single was causing a British furore Mick Jagger went and saw the British star, Cliff Richard, at London's Palladium Theatre. Cliff had himself caused media astonishment and general British breakfast-time amazement with reports of his appearing on stage with American evangelist Billy Graham in June 1966, and an agonized fan wrote in the pop paper, *Disc*. 'He's not the type to take up religion.'

Mick Jagger told Peter Jones:
He's very good . . . But I could never do it. You see the Shadows [Cliff's backing group and hit-makers in their own right] doing Russian dances all over the place. Can you honestly see us doing anything like that. It's just not our scene. And the fancy costume and the funny lines they have to speak . . .

A few weeks later, police raided the home of Keith Richard in West Wittering and this for some people was the greatest gift from the gods imaginable. Mick and Keith were arraigned before the courts for possession of drugs. The eventual outcome when the procedures of British justice had run their course was the quashing of the duo's conviction by the High Court after they had been sentenced to three years' and one year's imprisonment respectively.

In many quarters, including more responsible sections of the British press, there was a feeling that the Stones had been deliberately persecuted by various law-enforcement bodies, and that there had been the intent to make an example of them from which young people generally would learn how society proposed to deal with its supposed offenders.

Musically, change was afoot in the Stones' camp, as reflected in the 1967 album *Their Satanic Majesties*. With outward change came also internal squabbles.

These largely centred around the diminishing role of Brian Jones and the gradual ascendancy and almost total control within the Stones of the Richard—Jagger partnership. Yet this was inevitable with Brian slowly disintegrating as a person.

Their Satanic Majesties came clothed in a cover containing a three-dimensional colour photograph of the group. The Stones stood colourfully dressed against a somewhat surrealistic background.

However, the movement by the Stones on this album into electronic sounds did not please many fans and critics. Some said the Stones were attempting a Beatles' *Sgt Pepper* under the axiom, 'Anything they can do, we can do better'; but from the vantage point of the '70s, it's been said by many writers that the album was severely underestimated.

Norman Jopling in *Record Mirror* (16 December 1967) wrote that the album showed that the Stones could appeal to a more discriminating record market without isolating the younger fans.

Whatever the case, white R&B was losing its popularity in Britain and the Stones were to some degree caught up in the general flower-power, psychedelic ethos of that time. More musical change came within the next twelve months, as the album of December, 1968, *Beggars Banquet*, clearly showed.

People liked *Beggars Banquet* and saw it more akin to the Stones of old. The *New York Times* reviewer said 'The Beatles were still searching—and it showed', whilst he thought the Stones 'had found out where they were, and were building'.

Certainly it was an exciting disc, full of fast and furious rhythms, provocative songs, fine musicianship and Jagger on top vocal form. The earthiness had returned.

One new element had crept into the Rolling Stones' life of 1967–8. This was film. They had been filmed at work in the studio under the directorship of the famous Jean-Luc Godard. At first entitled *One Plus One*, the film was later named *Sympathy For The Devil* (which was the opening cut of *Beggars Banquet).* Mick had become the star of *Performance* and the group had been stars of a TV spectacular, Rock and Roll Circus.

More important in the Stones' latest musical trip was their return to music which could be performed, in contrast with the Beatles who had gradually grown away from material easily presentable live.

Mick was still Marianne Faithfull's boyfriend and in May 1969 both were charged with possessing cannabis. Not long after this, what had been pending for a long time became reality: Brian Jones left the Stones and was replaced by Mick Taylor. None of the group, however, expected the dramatic news of 3 July, which was that Brian Jones had died. Two days later at an open-air concert in London's Hyde Park, the Stones paid their tribute to him. Another era was over.

Left: Away from crowds, Brian Jones relaxes with Suki Poiter. Bottom left: Caught at a good musical moment. Often, for arranged pictures, the Stones were reputed to scowl deliberately. Here, for once, they are caught smiling.
Right: Record cover of *Their Satanic Majesties*; originally it was released in 3-dimensional colour.
Inset: On trial for suspected drug possession. They emerge walking tall.

In 1969 Mick was offered the part of Ned Kelly in a film portraying the Australian outlaw. For some people, the next months saw Mick Jagger change considerably in character. They felt he became obsessed with his image and one consequence was his sudden disinterest in the group's business affairs. Mick by now was very much the focal point of the group, although in some respects even if he hadn't wanted this, it was forced upon him.

The Stones had almost ceased operation. Albums were becoming once-a-year affairs and after August 1967 there was no single until May 1968, and then over a year before the excellent 'Honky Tonk Women' in July of 1969. They ceased being on the road. It very much needed at least one of the group to pull the band together again before the ease of upper-income-bracket living forever spoiled their hunger for an audience.

Jagger was the person to do this and he also had personal motivation in so doing. The period from late '68 to mid '69 had promised much but things had gone sour. There was the already mentioned lack of enthusiasm, apart from someone like Norman Jopling, for *Their Satanic Majesties* and Mick's film escapades were hardly successful. *Performance* was held up by distribution problems over some of its story and consequent scenes, and there was scant praise for Mick's portrayal of Ned Kelly.

And so in the autumn a tour of America was planned. A film would be made of the event. Whilst in America Mick was approached by Jerry Garcia of The Grateful Dead with the suggestion that the Stones should play a free concert near the tour's end somewhere in California. Mick saw it as a great finale for the film.

The venue, after much squabbling amongst those involved outside of the Stones' camp, became Altamont. It was a disastrous occasion and was to an extent the reason for a further time lapse in Rolling Stones activities. The film, *Altamont* or *Gimme Shelter*, records all. There were bad vibes amongst many in the crowd, many of whom were well laced with drugs and alcohol. There were several nasty sorties on the stage while other artists were playing, particularly during the set by Jefferson Airplane.

Mick arrived in red velvet cape and cap and, although he had been

Right: The occasion is festive though the group look thoughtful. At British Independent Television studios at Wembley, they record a special programme called Rock 'n' Roll Circus which also featured other famous rock stars including The Who, Eric Clapton and John Lennon. Inset: Mr and Mrs Jones and family at funeral service for Brian.

obsessed in past months by the idea of being assassinated by a wild fan or foe, he gave the impression of being in command. He presumably remained unperturbed by more sinister portents. For many rock fans on the American West Coast, star signs pointed out the day's menu: with the moon in Scorpio, violence and chaos were predicted.

And so it was. Even the more bizarre Jesus kids knew the score; for them, Mick and the Stones were at one with the devil, Lucifer, and there was the Stones' song called 'Sympathy for the Devil'.

The violent climax came with the murder of Meredith Hunter, aged eighteen. At one point he had a gun. Whether it was aimed at Mick Jagger no one will ever know. Suffice to say, Jagger saw it.

Altamont lived with the Stones for some time. It even seemed possible there would be no future Rolling Stones. However, some eighteen months later the Stones came out of hibernation and toured Britain in the spring of 1971. They had left Decca and formed their own concern with distribution via the more progressively orientated Kinney National Company group and the famous Marshall Chess, son of Chess Records' founder, Leonard, was placed in charge.

Their first new single for several years was issued: 'Brown Sugar'. The old flair was there. It was vintage Stones. The song sold. It was a Number One almost everywhere it was issued throughout the world.

Their first new album (as opposed to constant re-issues of old recordings of material made in Decca days), *Sticky Fingers*, was also a chart topper. Mick Jagger, who had parted from Marianne early in 1971, now married Bianca Perez Moreno de Macias, and moved with the Stones to France to avoid the British taxation system taking much of their earnings.

1972 saw the Stones back in America with an amazingly successful tour, chronicled in the book *A Journey through America with The Rolling Stones* by Robert Greenfield. Wherever they played they met with love and devotion.

The group gave notice that their tempestuous days were not over in issuing the *Goat's Head Soup* album of 1973. It contained the track, 'Star', which contained reference to groupies' activities, and many radio stations refused it airplay.

It came out one day prior to the Stones' undertaking probably their most extensive tour since 1967. They were touring Britain for the first time in two years, plus undertaking a vast itinerary of Western Europe, and for the first time in six years efforts were being made to find gigs behind the Iron Curtain.

Musically there was change, for on stage they added support from key-boardman, Billy Preston and sidesmen Bobby Keys, Jim Price and Trevor Lawrence. And for stage effect the Stones hired American expert Chip Monck for his fourth Stones' tour.

Those in music quarters who busied themselves writing that the Stones were past it were merely displaying their own senility. True, the Stones of old were no more—that era had ended at Altamont. The 1971–2 period had seen the tentative birth cries of a new Stones and in 1973, particularly before

Above: The Stones play at Altamont, possibly the most dramatic concert in rock history. Right: A loving moment between the extraordinary hussles surrounding Mick's marriage to Bianca. Below: Mick made up for his role in *Performance*, a twilight world of male–female identity.

...0 people at London's Wembley
...um, there was the new Stones
...d running through adolescence
...manhood. Their entire perform-
...was magnificent.
...ow they played plain, good, hon-
...ck 'n' roll, only better than any
... in the world. British music critic
... Dallas, writing some months
...ous to the epic events of '73 in the
...azine, *Let It Rock*, said (December
...2):

...if they lay off the demonic stuff, and
concentrate on simple horny material like 'Exile' and 'Honky Tonk
Women' they will escape assassina-
tion. But, in so doing, they have
stopped being the band we used to
rave over. The music has changed,
the personnel has changed, and
there will be more and more brilliant
hangers-on to blur the image.

Only the name has been un-
changed to protect the innocent.

Friday, 7 September, at Wembley
surely satisfied everyone but the manic
depressive.

Whilst the Stones were busily as-
sembling themselves into an incredible
funky rock 'n' roll band, Mick Jagger
continued to make headlines. Now
that he was of further interest, a father
safely married with a daughter, news-
papermen and photographers hunted
for some sign of dissension in the
Jagger household. The gossips were

continually at work as they reported Bianca dancing with Ryan O'Neal, the Stateside actor from *Love Story*, and David Bowie. Jagger expressed himself clearly on this point, 'She can dance with whom she likes, and so can I. If she dances with people, I don't mind.'

Jagger had also reached 30. He agreed with David Wigg of Britain's *Daily Express* that 'it's a dangerous age for some people.' And in the interview printed in the paper's edition for Tuesday, 23 August, the singer did not agree the Stones had become acceptable. He instanced problems faced in playing in Japan, Australia and even some parts of America.

1974 saw more books on the Stones and Mick Jagger. One of them by Anthony Scaduto, *Mick Jagger* (published in Britain by W. H. Allen), led to the Stones' vocalist saying Marianne Faithfull had told the author a number of lies about him and his life.

It was a quiet year apart from Mick Taylor saying he was leaving the group and rumours of Ron Wood and others joining the other four. There was the release of the album *It's Only Rock 'n' Roll* and fresh recordings were made near the end of 1974.

1975 meant the first tour of America for the Stones since 1972. On Labour Day, 1 May, a press conference for the purposes of outlining their tour was

Left: In concert, US 1975. Below: Poster for Made In The Shade. Bottom: Press handout for US tour, 1975, showing left to right, Keith Richard, Bill Wyman, Mick Jagger, Ollie Brown, Ron Wood, Billy Preston and Charlie Watts.

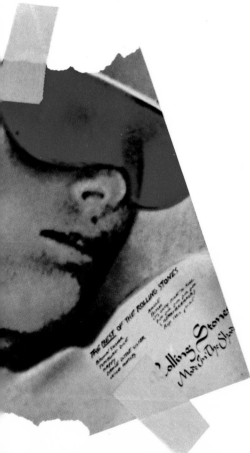

held at Feathers, on New York City's 10th Street and 5th Avenue. The Stones were not present. They were rolling down the city's 5th Avenue on a flat-topped truck made ready for a live concert, only this one physically moved.

A compilation Stones album was issued for the whetting of appetites in America, though the disc *Made In The Shade* was also released in Britain. The tracks came from previous releases and were favourites amongst the Stones' following. There was the familiar 'Brown Sugar' from the *Sticky Fingers* album, the first LP issued on the Stones' own label.

'Tumblin' Dice' and 'Happy' came from the album *Exile On Main Street* with 'Happy' being one of the few tracks which featured Keith Richard on vocal. The last Stones album provided 'Dance Little Sister' and then came the fine 'Wild Horses', a song previously recorded by the Flying Burrito Brothers with other versions in existence by Labelle, Melanie, and Leon Russell. Side two opened with 'Angie' from the *Goat's Head Soup* collection and was followed by 'Bitch', the B side of 'Brown Sugar'. 'It's Only Rock 'n Roll' was the third track and one of the half dozen tracks the Stones used from coast to coast. The others were 'Luxury', 'Ain't Too Proud To Beg', 'Fingerprint File', 'If You Can't Rock Me' and the above-mentioned, 'Dance Little Sister'. 'Doo Doo Doo Doo (Heartbreaker)' and 'Rip This Joint' concluded the LP, the latter being one of five numbers from *Exile on Main Street* featured on the tour.

The Stones' American tour bore the grand title of The Rolling Stones Tour of the Americas '75. It was three months in length.

At its halfway mark the Stones had performed before half a million people in eighteen concerts. At Cleveland, Ohio, they achieved a world record for attendance at a rock concert with controlled ticket sale. 83,000 fans heard them.

Ron Wood of Faces fame accompanied the Stones and thus provided the guitar licks missing after the departure of Mick Taylor. There was also the familiar talent of Billy Preston on keyboards with Ollie Brown on percussion.

All save seven dates were performed at indoor stadiums or halls with two long stays made at the Madison Square Gardens 22–27 June and the Inglewood Forum, Los Angeles.

The tour opened at the San Antonio Center, San Antonio, Texas. Amongst the cities covered were Milwaukee, Buffalo, Philadelphia, Memphis, Detroit, Atlanta and from Jacksonville, Florida, the tour had moved into Mexico and Brazil with a final concert at Caracas, Venezuela.

One major facet of the British '73 tour remained, some excellent staging,

lighting and sound, which clothed itself around two different stages. One of these was used in every city bar in New York and Los Angeles, the other at these long-stay stops. The first was transported in three semi-trucks, the stage weighing ten tons and measuring 71 feet in diameter. The New York and Los Angeles stage weighed 25 tons and needed an extra three semi-trucks.

The lighting system exaggerated the size of the performer and at the same time light seemed to move around the stage with the performers. The flying sound system was portable and consisted of a veritable battery of 32 cabinets weighing 500 lbs individually and eight tons collectively.

The band's equipment was transported around the States with a crew of 22 and a motor cavalcade of seven semi-trucks, with an extra truck provided for additional PA gear needed for an open-air concert.

By the end of the tour the Stones had played to nearly two million people. From the financial angle the event was staggering with some $50 million being taken and the Stones expecting a personal gross of $11 million.

The media, particularly the press, injected critical analysis into their commentary on the Stones' travelling show as it made its way through America. The old familiar statements were made and none expressed them better than Steve Dunleavy of the colourful *National Star* (21 June 1975).

Dunleavy wrote:
We have this pale-faced foreigner, this Englishman, getting $10 a seat from our kids to see him perform. And what do they see? They are blitzkrieged by a tightly packaged excess of four letter words and tacky smut . . . Here is this person, a convicted drug offender, preaching the gospel according to Jagger to our teenagers. Here is this person who spits on free-enterprise society but shuns his native country of England to live in France so he can avoid taxes . . . And here we are filling his pockets.

For writer Robert Christagau, the Stones of '75 were still flaunting the old sex themes, whatever the music might be and these were 'sex as power, sex as love, sex as pleasure, distance, craziness, release'.

Whatever the Stones do or did in their music or actions may be interpreted in a variety of ways, and there is no doubt that they have challenged the established views of society, with their desire to lead their *own* lives.

Despite what the press in its many guises said, however, for the fans of 1975 America there were similar feelings to those expressed way back in 1963 Richmond. For them, the Stones were and are the greatest.

FLASHBACK

MONTH BY MONTH, YEAR BY YEAR

Brian, Keith, Mick and Ian Stewart got together for the purpose of making good music at the Bricklayers' Arms. On Boxing Day 1962 the Rolling Stones (as yet unnamed) had a booking at the Piccadilly Club. Early in 1963 due to a BBC recording for the Alexis Korner Band, they deputized at the Marquee Club. Then followed various bookings at the Marquee and the Eel Pie Island Club, Ealing. At the IBC studios, Portland Place, London, various recording sessions were held. In February the Rolling Stones commenced an eight-month residency in Richmond, Surrey, at the Crawdaddy Club, Station Hotel.

Below: Andrew 'Loog' Oldham, Brian Jones and Keith Richard in an early recording session. Andrew Oldham signed up the Stones in April 1963.
Far right: A typical feature of any Stones' concert is the frenzy of the audience; a screaming fan attempts to touch her idol.

1963

APRIL

13 *Richmond and Twickenham Times* print first press story.

28 Andrew Oldham and Eric Easton see the Rolling Stones and sign a management deal the following day. The IBC tapes are bought for £90.

MAY

10 First official recording session. It takes place at the Olympic Studios, Barnes. Andrew Oldham produces; tracks include 'Come On' and 'I Wanna Be Loved'.

JUNE

7 'Come On' with 'I Wanna Be Loved' on the flip side released and the Rolling Stones make their first television appearance on British Independent Television's Thank your Lucky Stars.

13 First national daily newspaper coverage in the *Daily Mirror* by Patrick Doncaster. He describes their music as exciting.

SEPTEMBER

29 First English tour and on the same bill as the Everly Brothers and Bo Diddley. The tour commences at London's New Victoria cinema. The tour has 30 dates and concludes 3 November.

NOVEMBER

1 The single 'I Wanna Be Your Man' with B side 'Stoned' issued.

1964

JANUARY

6 Rolling Stones top the bill for the first time and with the Ronnettes begin touring. Marty Wilde is also billed and the first date is scheduled to take place at the Granada cinema, Harrow.

FEBRUARY

21 Release of single 'Not Fade Away' backed with 'Little By Little'. The A side was formerly recorded by Buddy Holly and the Crickets as the B side to 'Oh! Boy!' The B side of the Stones disc was written by Mick Jagger and Phil Spector. The latter plays maraccas.

APRIL

18 Rolling Stones take part in the Mad Mod Ball, which is held at the Empire Pool, Wembley.

20-21 Montreux: Stones at International TV Festival

22 *Daily Mirror* reports that the President of the National Federation of Hairdressers had described one of the Stones as having a hairstyle resembling a feather duster.

26 *New Musical Express* Poll Winners' Concert at Wembley. The album *The Rolling Stones* is released.

MAY

1 Jack Hutton, Editor, *Melody Maker*, as guest columnist for the *Daily Mirror*, reports on the Rolling Stones' visit to San Antonio, Texas, and comments on the group, 'As if by a pre-arranged signal, all five simultaneously pulled down the skin under their eyes and pushed up their noses. Believe me, it's frightening . . .'

10 Jimmy Savile, famous British DJ, talks about the Rolling Stones in his newspaper column in the Sunday *People* and says, 'The Stones are a great team for having a laugh and dress very clean and smart when they relax, contrary to what lots of people think . . .'

12 The Rolling Stones are refused admittance to a Bristol hotel because they are not wearing ties.

Above: The Stones first US tour—here they are given flowers and cake— June 1964.

27 The Headmaster of Woodlands Comprehensive School, Coventry, gains British press headlines. He says boys may have hair cut in Beatles fashion but not like Mick Jagger. Eleven M. Jagger-styled haircut boys suspended.

JUNE

3 The group's first American tour opens and continues until 20 June. The tour is broken when the group flies back to Magdalen College, Oxford, for a Commemoration Ball. The group had been booked a year previously for £100 ($250) and the college refused to relinquish the contract. They have paid ball-attenders desiring the Stones' presence. The Stones return at a cost of £1,500 ($3,750). The

ford.

16-17 The Stones fly to West Germany for Berlin TV show.

18-21 Belgium TV dates and on the 20th the Stones play at the famous Olympia, Paris. Riots occur in streets after show and 150 arrests made.

23 The Stones fly to America for twelve-date tour and two special occasions, at the Academy of Music and the Ed Sullivan Show.

28-29 They film for the Tami Awards TV show and meet Billy J. Kramer and the Dakotas plus Gerry and the Pacemakers.

NOVEMBER

2 They record for Jack Good's Shindig TV show. Their co-manager has pneumonia and flies back to Britain.

5 They record at the famous Chess studios in Chicago.

13 Release in the UK (while they are still in the States) of 'Little Red Rooster' and 'Off The Hook'.

23 The group find themselves banned by BBC after arriving late for radio shows Top Gear and Saturday Club.

27 Tettenhall Court, Staffordshire. Mick Jagger is fined £16 ($40) for driving offences.

29 Stones annoy some people by refusing to appear at an ABC TV press reception held in Birmingham.

DECEMBER

21 Publication of pocket book *Ode to a High-flying Bird* by Charlie Watts. (It had been written in 1961 and was the story of Charlie 'Bird' Parker.)

concert performance was poor.

23 Official return from the States and tumultuous reception at London's Heathrow Airport. There are riots.

26 The single 'It's All Over Now' and 'Good Times, Bad Times' issued.

JULY

4 The group appear as panellists on BBC TV's Juke Box Jury and are not reviewed kindly by the general British press.

8 'It's All Over Now' hits Number One in the charts. Beatles have a party for the premiere of *A Hard Day's Night* at London's plush Dorchester Hotel and Keith, Bill and Brian attend.

24 The group play the Empress Ballroom, Blackpool. Fans cause riots and the group flees from stage. Damage estimated at several thousands of pounds.

AUGUST

3 The group star at the Third Pop Concert held at Longleat House, home of the Marquess of Bath. Crowd estimated at 25,000.

7 The Rolling Stones play the National Jazz and Blues Festival held at Richmond, Surrey.

8 Concert at The Hague — audience gets out of hand and several girls suffer clothes damage.

10 Manchester, Belle Vue, New Elizabethan Ballroom. Fifty policemen are needed to keep order. Two policewomen are reported as fainting cases. No one can say whether in admiration for the group or because of general warmth of atmosphere.

13 7,000 people hear the Stones at the Ballroom, Douglas, Isle of Man.

14 'Five By Five' EP released to advance order

of over 200,000.

18 Stones do a quick tour of the Channel Islands.

SEPTEMBER

5 British tour commences at the Astoria cinema, Finsbury Park, which in the '70s became The Rainbow and venue of many large rock occasions featuring numerous famous singers and bands. The Mojos, Charlie and Inez Fox accompany the Stones. In *Melody Maker* the group is voted the most popular rock group and in the best song category the award goes to 'Not Fade Away'.

OCTOBER

9 The Stones announce they will not be touring South Africa.

14 Charlie Watts marries Shirley Ann Shepherd. The wedding is held in Brad-

1965

JANUARY

6–8 Tour of Ireland.

13 Film item recorded for Thank Your Lucky Stars TV show.

15 Ready, Steady, Go! T.V. show. Second Stones album issued.

17 Flight to Los Angeles for recording work.

21 Stones arrive in Sydney for Roy Orbison tour. Rioting at airport from welcoming committee of around 3,000 fans.

30 Australian tour ends.

FEBRUARY

1–8 Tour of New Zealand.

10–13 Stones return to Australia.

16–17 In Singapore and Hong Kong with the Hollies.

26 Release of 'The Last Time' and 'Play With Fire'. Mick gets mobbed on TV show Ready, Steady, Go!

MARCH

5 Major English tour commences and also on the bill are the Hollies and Dave Berry.

26 Scandinavian tour commences. The Stones also record for TV.

APRIL

2 End of Scandinavian tour.

9 The group perform live on Ready, Steady, Go!

11 At Wembley, the Stones at *New Musical Express* Poll Winners' Concert.

13–16 German shows and TV.

17–18 Paris, Olympia.

22 Canadian and American tour until 29 May and the group fly to Montreal.

MAY

2 Ed Sullivan TV show.

10–11 Recording at Chess studios, Chicago.

12–13 Recording at RCA studios in Los Angeles.

20 Recording for Shindig TV show with Jack Good.

JUNE

10 BBC TV Top of the Pops.

11 Issue of EP 'Got Love If You Want It'.

12 Record for Thank Your Lucky Stars.

15-18 Short Scottish tour.

24-29 Scandinavian tour. Rioting fans in Oslo, Norway.

29 Charlie buys house once owned by Archbishop of Canterbury, a sixteenth-century residence, Hallands, in Sussex.

JULY

1 A Glasgow magistrate attacks the Stones in a case concerned with fans who had broken a shop window.

7 Los Angeles. More recording sessions at RCA.

16 Short British tour, and at Exeter's Odeon the Walker Brothers also feature on the bill.

22 Bill, Brian and Mick each fined £5 ($12) for insulting behaviour at a filling station on 18 March.

AUGUST

1 Stones at the London Palladium.

20 Release of 'I Can't Get No Satisfaction' with B side 'The Spider And The Fly'. Already the disc is a million-seller in the United States.

23 Security guards hose down Stones fans outside Manchester television studios.

24 The Hilton Hotel, London, and a first meeting of the Stones with Allen Klein.

28 Andrew Oldham and Allen Klein announced as the group's co-managers. They sign a new five-year contract with Decca. Decca will finance their first film.

SEPTEMBER

3-5 Ireland.

8 Stones announce last ballroom appearance and play at Douglas, Isle of Man.

Left: The Stones on Ready, Steady, Go! Inset: The Band arrive in Stockholm, June 1965. Overleaf: Ready, Steady, Go! 1965.

10 The group star in their own edition of Ready, Steady, Go!

11-17 German and Austrian tour. Riots during tour and Berlin Hilton cancels Stone hotel bookings.

24 Beginning of British tour. Spencer Davis, Mike Sarne and John Leyton on same billing. During month issue of LP *Out Of Our Heads*.

OCTOBER

22 Release of single 'Get Off Of My Cloud'/'The Singer Not The Song'.

29 To Montreal and fourth Canadian/American tour until 5 December.

DECEMBER

3 At Sacramento, Keith knocked unconscious by electric shock.

31 Appear on a Rediffusion TV special, The New Year Starts Here.

1966

FEBRUARY

4 Release of '19th Nervous Breakdown' backed with 'As Tears Go By'. The latter had been a hit for Marianne Faithfull in August 1964.

13 Ed Sullivan TV show recording in New York.

14 To Sydney, Australia, for tour which also includes appearances in New Zealand.

MARCH

26 European tour commences and runs until 5 April. Mick receives eight stitches after being hit by chair thrown onto stage.

APRIL

15 Issue of LP *Aftermath*.

MAY

1 *New Musical Express* Poll Winners' Concert.

13 TV and Thank Your Lucky Stars. Announcement of first Stones film *Only Lovers Left Alive*. Release of 'Paint It Black' coupled with 'Long Long Awhile'.

27 Another appearance on Ready, Steady, Go!

JUNE

14 Mick collapses from exhaustion.

21 The group sue fourteen hotels over a booking ban in New York for £1,750,850 ($4,377,125) because hotels turned down bookings. A damages suit also filed saying the hotels had injured the group's reputation and that the refusal of bookings was a 'discrimination on account of national origin' and violated New York's civil rights laws.

23 Rolling Stones arrive in New York for fifth American/Canadian tour, ending 28 July in Hawaii.

AUGUST

3 They begin a two-week recording schedule at the RCA studios in Los Angeles.

7 First British showing of their package film, *Gather No Moss*.

10 Double TV billing for the Stones, in America they appear on the Ed Sullivan show and in England on Ready, Steady, Go!

12 Tour opens in Münster, Germany—fans riot.

16 In the British parliament, Tom Driberg MP asks the house to deplore the action of a magistrate who had called the Stones 'complete morons' and said they wore 'filthy clothes'.

23 Release of 'Have You Seen Your Mother Baby?' coupled with 'Who's Driving Your Plane?' At the opening of their British tour the Stones find themselves presented with 20 gold discs. The tour opens at London's Royal Albert Hall. Also on the bill are Ike and Tina Turner and the Yardbirds.

OCTOBER

9 British tour ends.

29 US tour opens in Montreal.

NOVEMBER

Release of two albums. One is a compilation of hits and called *Big Hits* (*High Tide And Green Grass*) and the other a new LP, *Got Live If You Want It*, a live recording of the Albert Hall concert.

DECEMBER

10 In *NME* polls, the Rolling Stones are top British Rhythm and Blues group, and the best song of the year is 'Satisfaction'.

Above: Tom Driberg, British MP friend of Mick Jagger.

Top: A row at the London Palladium. Above: In Warsaw. Right: Keith Richard 'dressed' for the Beggars Banquet celebration, December 1968.

1967

JANUARY

13 New York, Ed Sullivan show.

20 Release of LP, *Between The Buttons*.

22 Considerable consternation when Stones refuse to go on the traditional revolving stage with the show's stars at national TV show, London Palladium.

28 Release of 'Let's Spend The Night Together' and B side 'Ruby Tuesday'. Outcry over supposed meaning of A side and whether the Stones were suggesting one went to bed with the other rather than go home . . . During month British release of *Between The Buttons*. That title also annoys some people.

FEBRUARY

2 London, on recorded Top Of The Pops.

6 Mick Jagger announces he is taking action against the British Sunday newspaper, *News of the World*.

12 Keith Richard's home at West Wittering is raided by the police.

19 *News of the World* headlines, 'Drug Squad Raids Pop Stars' Party'.

MARCH

9 Brian Jones goes into hospital with respiratory trouble.

25 Opening of European tour in Sweden at Orebro and tour lasts until 17 April.

APRIL

8 Newspaper headlines for British Olympic gold medallist Lyn Davies. He makes critical remarks about the Stones' behaviour and the accusations are denied by Mick

38

Jagger. Jagger says, 'They [the hotel's public rooms] were crammed with athletes behaving badly.'

13 First visit for Stones behind the Iron Curtain as they go to Warsaw. 3,000 students storm the Palace of Culture and police use batons and tear gas.

24 Cannes Film Festival contains a German entry *A Degree of Murder* with music by Brian Jones and starring his girlfriend Anita Pallenberg.

MAY

10 Keith and Mick are arraigned before the court for the drug offences of 12 February and sent for trial at the West Sussex Quarter Sessions. Brian Jones is charged with being in possession of Indian hemp at his South London flat.

12 *New Musical Express* Poll Winners' Concert at London's Wembley.

21 Mick appears on a BBC programme, Look of the Week, and discusses the relationships between audiences and performers.

JUNE

Decca issue the Stones' *Flowers* album.

29 Mick and Keith are found guilty of drug charges at the West Sussex Quarter Ses-

sions. Keith is given one year in gaol and Mick three.

30 The two are given bail in the High Court.

JULY

1 The British newspaper *The Times* astounds many, delights others with an editorial of some length called 'Butterfly on a Wheel' which is sympathetic towards the Stones.

6 Brian Jones goes into hospital suffering from exhaustion.

31 At appeal courts the Lord Chief Justice quashes Keith Richard's conviction and gives Mick a conditional discharge.

AUGUST

18 Release of a single with Lennon and McCartney on backing harmonies called 'We Love You'. The disc is described as a thank-you to fans for their support and sympathy during the various drug-charge problems of past months.

26 Weekend of Brian Epstein's death. Mick Jagger and Marianne Faithfull leave to go and visit the famous Maharishi.

SEPTEMBER

Stones go to America and around the end of the month it is learnt that they have broken away from Andrew Oldham and that from now on they will be responsible for producing their own records.

OCTOBER

31 Brian Jones receives nine-month prison sentence for possessing cannabis but is later released on bail pending appeal.

DECEMBER

8 *Their Satanic Majesties* issued.

12 Brian Jones finds his gaol sentence set aside and he receives three years' probation and a £1,000 ($2,500) fine.

15 Brian collapses from overstrain and is admitted to St George's Hospital, London.

16 Announcement that the Stones will launch their own record label with the probable title of *Mother Earth*.

1968

JANUARY

4 According to British newspaper, the *Daily Sketch*, the University of California in Los Angeles demands a study of Rolling Stones music for all students intending to take a music degree.

MARCH

2 Stones engage Jimmy Miller as a producer.

15 First recording sessions held with Jimmy Miller.

18 Serafina Watts born to Charlie and Shirley.

MAY

12 First live appearance by the Stones in Britain for two years at the *New Musical Express* Poll Winners' Concert.

21 Brian Jones arrested and charged with possession of cannabis. He is given bail.

25 Release of 'Jumpin' Jack Flash' coupled with 'Child Of The Moon'.

31 Announcement that the Rolling Stones are making a film with Jean-Luc Godard entitled *One Plus One*.

JUNE

11 Brian Jones committed for trial and whilst the

group records at Olympic studios there is a fire but no one injured.

29 Mick Jagger begins filming *Performance*.

JULY

4 American single 'Street Fighting Man' banned by some.

SEPTEMBER

6 Mick is a guest on the David Frost TV show (in Britain).

26 Brian Jones is found guilty and fined.

NOVEMBER

21 A. A. Milne's old home bought by Brian Jones. This is Cotchford Farm, Hartfield, Sussex, where Winnie the Pooh books were written.

DECEMBER

5 The Stones hold a 'beggars' banquet' at London's Elizabethan Rooms to mark the release of album *Beggars Banquet*.

12 Rolling Stones Rock 'n' Roll Circus is filmed at Wembley studios for Independent Television. Among the 'friends' are John Lennon and Yoko Ono.

18 Mick and Marianne, Keith and Anita leave for a Brazilian holiday.

1969

JANUARY

17 In Lima, Mick and Keith are asked to leave the Hotel for wearing op art trousers and nothing else. They move to the exclusive Hotel Bolivar.

MAY

24 Mick and Marianne charged in London for possession of cannabis and given bail.

28 It is announced that Mick will play Ned Kelly in the film about this Australian hero.

JUNE

8 Brian Jones leaves the Stones. Mick Taylor replaces him.

13 A photo call is held in London's Hyde Park to introduce Mick Taylor.

JULY

3 Brian Jones dies at his home, Cotchford Farm, Hartfield, Sussex.

5 Hyde Park, London, and a free concert by the Rolling Stones.

6 Mick Jagger leaves for his Australian filming of *Ned Kelly*. Marianne's husband sues her for divorce.

Right: Hyde Park Concert, July 1969. Below: Altamont, December 1969.

10 Brian Jones is buried at his home town, Cheltenham.

11 Release of 'Honky Tonk Women'/'You Can't Always Get What You Want'.

AUGUST

10 Keith Richard becomes a 'dad' and names his son Marlon.

18 During filming of *Ned Kelly*, Mick is accidentally shot in the hand.

SEPTEMBER

10 Announcement of forthcoming autumn tour of the States.

12 Mick returns from Australia. The LP *Through The Past Darkly* is issued.

OCTOBER

17 The Stones arrive in LA to set up their next American tour. It will open on 7 November.

DECEMBER

6 Famous Altamont concert in which a member of the audience was alleged to have attempted to assassinate Mick.

14 The group plays London's Saville Theatre.

19 Mick Jagger fined for possession of cannabis whilst Marianne is acquitted.

21 Gig at the Lyceum, London. Fans covered with artificial snow as part of this Christmas party show.

1970

JANUARY

31 The Stones file a £4,580,000 ($11,350,000) lawsuit against Sears Point International Raceway for breach of contract and fraud and say that at the last minute they were forced to move to Altamont Raceway, some 40 miles away, for their 6 December concert.

JULY

28 *Ned Kelly* is premiered in Melbourne, Australia.

30 The Stones inform Allen Klein that neither he nor ABKCO Industries Inc. nor anyone else have the right to negotiate future recordings.

AUGUST

1 The film *Performance* is released in London.

29 The group leaves for European tour which continues until 9 October.

SEPTEMBER

8 Release of 'Get Yer Ya-Yas Out'.

19 Release of *Performance* soundtrack LP.

23 Performance of group at Olympia, Paris.

OCTOBER

1 At Palazzo dello Sport, Milan, and wild, excited scenes.

7 Release of *Ned Kelly* in UK.

NOVEMBER

1 Issue of Mick's solo disc 'Memo To Turner'.

DECEMBER

6 New York: the film *Gimme Shelter* opens.

1971

JANUARY

4 Charity premiere in London of *Performance*, attended by Keith Richard.

MARCH

2 BBC Radio 4 programme devoted to the story of Brian Jones by Michael Wale given national hearing.

4 Stones announce they will set up home in France. They start their British tour at Newcastle-upon-Tyne.

14 At London's Roundhouse a farewell concert is held.

26 Stones give a farewell party at Skindles Hotel, Maidenhead, and John and Yoko are among the guests.

APRIL

1 Announcement that famous American recording manager, Marshall Chess, would run their record label which will be called Rolling Stones Records.

6 Stones sign a distribution deal with Kinney National.

13 First release under new aegis is a maxi single 'Brown Sugar', 'Bitch', 'Let It Rock'.

18 Mick and Bianca seen leaving the Yves Saint Laurent boutique and deny marriage is intended.

23 First album on new label is entitled *Sticky Fingers*. At around the same time Decca issue *Stone Age* which has four hitherto unreleased tracks on it.

MAY

2 Bianca's birthday. Mick buys her a £4,000 ($10,000) diamond bracelet and gives a dinner party and party for her at a hotel's private disco.

3 'Brown Sugar' already at Number One in the charts.

THE ROLLING STONES EUROPEAN TOUR 1970
A SBA PRESENTATION

8-9 Mick goes to Paris and collects two wedding rings which have been specially designed by one of the world-famous French jewellers.

11 Mr and Mrs Joe Jagger (Mick's parents) and friends leave London en route for St Tropez, in order to attend Mick's wedding.

12 Mick marries Bianca in a civil ceremony at the Town Hall in St Tropez; the marriage then blessed at the Chapel of St Anne. Among the guests are Paul and Linda, Ringo and Maureen; Ron Wood, Ronnie Lane, Ian Mc-Laglen and Kenny Jones, all of the Faces; Mr and Mrs Joe Jagger and Mick's brother, Chris, Jimmy Miller and Marshall Chess.

13 Mick and Bianca leave for their honeymoon in a yacht.

16 Mick and Bianca change yachts at Micinaggio, Corsica, and head for a château, which is accessible only from the sea.

JUNE

2 Mick and Bianca make for Venice.

JULY

2 Bill Wyman produces debut disc of Tucky Buzzard called 'She's A Striker'.

30 Passing through London's Heathrow airport, Mick and Bianca announce they are expecting a baby.

31 Premiere of *Gimme Shelter* at the Rialto Cinema, London.

AUGUST

5 British *Oz* magazine trial result. Jagger says a people or a generation cannot be shut off from what they wish to read.

20 *Howlin' Wolf* released on the Rolling Stones label with background accompaniment partly supplied by Bill Wyman and Charlie Watts.

27 Issue of *Gimme Shelter* LP by Decca.

SEPTEMBER

23 Mick and Bianca at a Johnny Halliday performance in Paris.

OCTOBER

1 Keith's French house broken into and thieves steal eleven guitars.

8 Rolling Stones Records release an album of Moroccan folk music recorded by Brian Jones.

21 A daughter, Jade, is born to Bianca and Mick at the Belvedere Nursing Home, Paris.

26 British ATV show, Beaton By Bailey, includes observations from Mick.

NOVEMBER

3 Pierre Cardin's Paris party for Alice Cooper attended by Mick and Bianca.

30 Keith and Mick leave for America and Keith makes a point of calling at Nashville where he is having guitars especially made up for him to replace the stolen ones.

Far left: Poster for 1970 European tour. Centre: Mick Jagger being made up for the filming of *Ned Kelly*. Below: Mick and Bianca on honeymoon in Venice, June 1971.

1972

FEBRUARY

1 Mick and Bianca attend wedding of former Mamas and Papas star, John Phillips, with Genevieve Waite.

15 Stones in Los Angeles, recording.

29 Mick goes to a Marc Bolan concert at Hollywood's Palladium.

APRIL

6 With Bianca and Jade, Mick stops at Sydney en route for Bali for three-week holiday. They return home on 24 April.

14 Release of 'Tumblin' Dice' and 'Sweet Black Angel'.

29 *New Musical Express* gives its readers a promotional record by the Rolling Stones. The disc gives people some taste of the forthcoming album.

MAY

5 Wilson Pickett has a reception at the Stones' record company's office and there to greet him are Bill Wyman and Charlie Watts.

9 Rolling Stones and ABKO Industries Inc. and Allen Klein jointly announce settlement of all their outstanding differences.

12 Release of LP *Exile on Main Street*.

21 Rehearsals commence for American tour.

23 Stones visit the American Embassy in London to collect their work permits. Only Bill actually catches the scheduled flight, the others miss it.

25 Mick, Keith and Mick Taylor leave for the States; Bianca says goodbye at the airport.

29 'Brown Sugar' hits Number 1 in the American charts, and *Sticky Fingers* is at the top place in the album listings.

JUNE

3 Opening concert of the American/Canadian tour (which continues until 26 July) is at Vancouver's Pacific Colloseum. 2,000 people attempt to gatecrash and 30 policemen, who are on duty at the concert, are injured.

13 At the San Diego concert 60 people get arrested and at least fifteen injuries are recorded.

14 Tucson, Arizona, sees more fans attempt to gatecrash a Stones concert. Police use tear gas to disperse around 300 young people.

15 Concert at the University of New Mexico, Albuquerque. There is a forged-ticket scare.

30 In London, Decca release a maxi single. One track is 'Street Fighting Man'. During June, *Exile On Main Street* causes British clean-up campaigner Mrs Mary Whitehouse to complain to the BBC about supposed obscenities on two tracks.

JULY

4 48,000 are at the Robert F. Kennedy Stadium in Washington DC for the Stones' concert. 61 are arrested.

17 Montreal, Forum. 3,000 fake tickets are discovered and it causes rioting. Stones suffer equipment damage from a bomb and replacements are flown from LA.

24 Stones play Madison Square Garden.

Above: Mick's 29th birthday celebration. He received a cake on stage during a concert at Madison Square Garden, New York, in July 1972. Right: Mick surveys the damage in Nicaragua. Opposite above left: Part of the Lex Hotel poster. Below left: Mick with his portrait by Cecil Beaton. Above right: Bianca modelling Yves Saint Laurent dress. Below right: Keith's house at West Wittering, on fire.

25 Stones play their second concert at Madison Square Garden.

26 Stones play their third Garden concert and it is

Mick's birthday. The occasion is marked by presentation of a cake and giant panda. At the end of the concert Mick throws rose petals and custard pies. A party is held afterwards.

AUGUST

10-11 Mick and Bianca attend the Oval Test cricket match.

11 Two thirds of the US Dick Cavett show is given over to the Stones.

28 Mick and Bianca holiday in Ireland.

SEPTEMBER

22 Shirley Arnold, personal secretary for nine years to the Stones, has a farewell party at the London WEA record company offices and Mick, Bianca, Charlie and Shirley Watts and Mick Taylor attend.

NOVEMBER

6 At Chelmsford Magistrates' Court, Bill Wyman is banned from driving and fined £20 ($45) for speeding in his Mercedes.

8 Bianca becomes 'Woman of the Year' in the category of 'hats' and receives her award at London's Inn on the Park.

22-4 Mick is in New York helping Yoko record an album with husband John Lennon.

25 Stones arrive in Jamaica to record for the *Goat's Head Soup* LP.

30 Mick, Keith and Mick Taylor fly to LA to record (also for *Goat's Head Soup*).

DECEMBER

4-5 Mick, Bill and Charlie fly from Nice to Jamaica and more recordings are made.

21 Completion of Jamaican recordings.

23 A serious earthquake in Nicaragua, Bianca's home country, and at Managua, her parents' town.

26 Mick and Bianca leave London's Heathrow for Nicaragua.

28 They take the final stage in their journey from Kingston, Jamaica, taking with them 2,000 typhoid injection capsules. While searching they find Bianca's mother, Señora Macias, and other members of her family.

1973

JANUARY

3 Mick and Bianca voted the best dressed man and woman of 1972 by an American poll of 2,000 international fashion editors and experts.

4 Mick and Bianca are missing for 48 hours in Nicaragua but worries turn to smiles as the couple make their safety known. An announcement is made that the Stones are banned from entering Australia, with no reason given.

9 Mr Albert Grassley of the Australian Immigration Ministry says the ban on the Rolling Stones group has been lifted.

10 Mick, now in LA, announces his wish to hold a benefit concert to provide funds for the Nicaraguan earthquake victims.

18 Over £200,000 ($500,000) is raised at the LA benefit concert.

21-22 Stones play at the International Sports Center, Honolulu.

FEBRUARY

8 Stones are in Australia.

9 A Stones press conference in Sydney.

11 Stones in Auckland and 30,000 people attend their concert at the Western Springs Stadium.

13 Stones are back in Australia and at Milton Park, Brisbane.

16 Stones in Melbourne and a press conference at the Montsaluat Castle.

20-21 Adelaide and concerts at Memorial Park Drive. Around 5,000 young people clash with police, and 21 people arrested.

24 Stones play at the Australian test match cricket ground at Perth.

26-7 Two concerts at the Royal Randwick racecourse, Sydney.

MARCH

26 An advertisement appears in the London *Times* depicting portraits of the Rolling Stones, Edward Heath, David Frost, Barbra Streisand and

Mark Spitz. The advertisement is for the new Lex Hotel at London's Heathrow. Mr Heath, then Prime Minister, complains about pictures of well-known personalities being used in advertisements without permission. Mick Jagger says that the Rolling Stones have no objection at standing beside Mr Heath and they hope the feeling is mutual.

APRIL

4 The issue of *Radio Times* (the British TV guide to BBC television and radio programmes with a huge sales figure) reproduces a colour photograph of Mick Jagger on the cover with inside copy on his parents and old friends.

7 The BBC commences its series entitled The Rolling Stones Story.

23 A report appears in the British National daily, the *Daily Express*, that Mick Jagger's portrait in oils by Sir Cecil Beaton will appear for sale at the famous Sotheby's salerooms.

29 Another oldie is released by the British Decca record company, 'Sad Day' coupled with 'You Can't Always Get What You Want'.

30 Mick and Bianca attend a special party in New York organized by the magazine *After Dark* at which Bette Middler receives an award as Entertainer of the Year.

MAY

2 Mick's portrait is sold to a private buyer for £220 ($550).

4 In Washington DC Mick and Bianca present the Senate with a cheque for £350,000 ($787,500) for the Pan American Development Fund. In turn they receive a Golden Key with grateful thanks for putting on the charity concert.

10 Mick's English home, Stargroves, catches fire but the extent of the damage is slight.

17 A new pop label is launched in Britain, GM records, and Mick attends the reception at the famous Ritz Hotel, London. Mick's brother Chris is one of the first to be signed up.

JUNE

6 GM-owner Billy Gaff throws a special London party, which the Jaggers attend, and there is storming of his house by fans.

13 America's *Creem* magazine votes the Stones number one group, number one live group and they receive the top album award for *Exile On Main Street*. Bill gets the top bass player award.

14 The Jimi Hendrix film opens in London and

one part of the film is conversations between Jimi and Mick.

18 Mick and Bianca go holidaying in Italy.

25 Mick hears Mick Taylor performing in Mike Oldfield's *Tubular Bells*.

JULY

4 David Bowie announces he is retiring from live concerts and Mick and Bianca attend a special dinner party at the Café Royal, London.

15 The Jaggers attend a pop concert at London's White City Stadium.

17 Announcement made of the Stones tour of Europe and the UK in the autumn.

24-25 Bianca models Yves Saint Laurent clothes for the British *Daily Mirror*.

26 Mick is 30.

30 Mick sees test match cricket at The Oval, London.

31 At West Wittering, Keith's house catches fire but no one is hurt. Some antique furniture, books and equipment are saved but the house is extensively damaged.

AUGUST

6 UK box offices open for forthcoming Stones tours and stories abound of fans queueing all night.

20 'Angie' and 'Silver Track' released on an EP in Britain as a trailer of the forthcoming album.

31 *Goat's Head Soup* is issued.

SEPTEMBER

1 Stones in Europe and their first tour for three years opens at the Stadthalle, Vienna. A representative from the Soviet Union's Ministry of Culture, Yuri Kurinoff, is present.

6 Stones are back in London and go partying at Blenheim Palace, near Oxford.

7 The first of three concerts at London's Empire Pool.

10 BBC Radio DJs on stations 1 and 2 are asked not to play 'Star star' from the *Goat's Head Soup* album.

11 British dates continue.

19 Last European date at Berlin.

24 Keith Richard fined for drug possession but he denies the offence and says they belonged to people who at various times resided at his house while he was away.

NOVEMBER

8 Stones record in Munich.

1974

JANUARY

5 Bill Wyman begins recording solo album and has with him, among others, Dr John and Leon Russell.

12 UK Atlantic issue 'Brown Sugar'/'Bitch'/'Let It Rock' in its Atlantic Gold series.

FEBRUARY

9 Books published on the Rolling Stones. Robert Greenfield writes *A Journey through America with the Rolling Stones*. Anthony Scaduto pens *Mick Jagger*.

APRIL

4 Premiere in America for *Ladies and Gentlemen, The Rolling Stones*.

JUNE

Keith Richard collaborates on Ron Wood's solo LP. Mick Jagger features on a Billy Preston album.

JULY

3 Brian Jones fans make a pilgrimage to his grave at Cheltenham on the sixth anniversary of his death.

6 British publication date of book on Mick by Jamake Mamake Highwater, otherwise known as J. Marks.

9 Stones appear on BBC TV's Old Grey Whistle Test.

13–14 Keith Richard appears with Ron Wood and guests at London's Kilburn State cinema.

20 The RPO collaborate on David Bedford's new album and Mick Taylor is scheduled to take part. Mick Jagger is in Madison Square, New York for Eric Clapton's concert.

23 A tour of America for Mick's brother, Chris, is announced.

26 Mick's birthday. Now 31. Release of Stones' new single 'It's Only Rock 'n' Roll'.

27 Mick has a birthday party in Chelsea. Rod Stewart, Pete Townshend and the late Mama Cass attend.

27 The O'Jays have issued the album *Live In London*; it was recorded with the aid of the Stones' mobile recording unit.

29 Bill Wyman and girlfriend Astrid Lundstrom rent a villa in Venice and await the building of a house to Bill's design.

AUGUST

3 Ron Wood's album *I've Got My Own Album To Do* with Rod Stewart and Mick as backing musicians is said to have 13 September release.

4 A Mick Taylor is found residing in high-class Hong Kong but turns out to be an impostor. His striking resemblance to the Stones even deceives newsmen. His name is given as Jonathan Kern.

7 Mick accuses Marianne Faithfull of telling lies about him in Anthony Scaduto's book.

8 BBC TV features the Stones.

10 Mick announces he has over 100 very early Stones tapes in his possession and aims to release a number within the next year.

17 Film of Stones' 1972 tour receives its premiere in LA and money goes towards the LA Free Clinic. Sources say Keith Richard joined the Ronnettes on stage at London's Bibas Rainbow room concert.

19 Reports suggest Mick offered lead in a film *Joe Bunch and All That Glitters*. Mick's part would be that of a con-man.

22 Mick says he would like to purchase a church as a recording studio.

30 Marianne Faithfull announces she will co-star in a Minardos-directed thriller, *Assault on Agathan*.

SEPTEMBER

1 BBC Radio One features Mick on its Top Twelve programme where an artist talks about his favourite twelve tracks and these are played.

7 Carole King and Dr John reported recording with Bill Wyman at Miami's Criteria studio.

8 Mick is featured on new Keith Moon album release, *Like A Rat Up A Pipe*.

13 Brondesbury Synagogue, London, is one possible location for Mick's sound recording studio.

15 Mick and Bianca in Hollywood. Mick wears an 'ice-cream' suit and denies he is about to do a film.

18 Mick rents from Andy Warhol a house at Montaux, Long Island. Bill Wyman's intention of flying to Kinshasa thwarted when the world heavyweight fight is cancelled.

OCTOBER

4 Rumours circulate of Mick being asked to run for British political office but denied by the Stones' LA office.

8 Bianca says that Mick married her because he looks rather like her.

10 San Francisco radio station says Mick has been shot. The Stones' London Press Office denies this.

17 Mick escorts Nathalie Delon in Paris for one week and rumours of romance quashed by Mick who reveals he will shortly be going to Barbados.

18 *It's Only Rock 'n' Roll* issued. Keith arranges dental appointments in Switzerland. Also he applies for permission to rebuild his 500-year-old moated farmhouse at West Wittering.

19 Bianca tears a cartilage whilst fishing with Mick and John Lennon on Long Island.

26 Mick and Bianca nearly get removed from a party thrown by Joe Levine after the opening night of *Night Porter*. Mrs Levine apparently thought Mick was scruffy but approved of his presence when she found out who he was.

30 Bianca is reported as saying in Jamaica that she had wanted to name her baby Jesse James and that she would have been pleased if born male.

NOVEMBER

15 Release of 'White Lightnin'' single from Bill Wyman.

17 Mick says the Stones will soon be back in the studios for new recordings.

23 Reports of Keith Richard being in the Verne Sinus Recording Studio where he had taped organ and vocals for a song called 'Scarlet'.

24 Bianca attends premiere at New York's Bacon Theater of *Sergeant Pepper's Lonely Hearts Club Band*.

DECEMBER

7 Stones in Munich for recordings. Mick and Bianca at Elton John's Thanksgiving party after his Madison Square Garden gig.

14 Mick Taylor says he will leave the Stones.

18 Keith Richard is 31.

23 Ron Wood denies he has been asked by Mick to join the Stones.

26 Mick and rest of Stones phone in from Germany to Whittington and Royal Northern Hospital patients in Radio Whittington's Hunky Chunky show.

28 London Records, former Stones label in USA, get ready for special sales drive since Stones' tenth anniversary is close. Seventeen Stones albums will be promoted under the slogan 'World's Greatest Rock 'n' Roll Band—A London Recording Where It All Began'.

30 Mick tells Britain's *Daily Express* that he is related to painter David Jagger.

Left: The group pose for photographers during recording at BBC TV studios, August 1974.

1975

JANUARY

4 Announcement of possible live gig album.

5 Mick in Nicaragua with Bianca.

17 Rumour of Mick Ronson joining Stones, denied by LA office.

18 Publication of George Tremlett's *Rolling Stones* book.

24 Mick is pictured in Paris being measured for new suits.

25 Keith Richard attends Doobie Bros reception.

27 Marianne Faithfull in hospital suffering from peritonitis.

FEBRUARY

1 Billy Preston says he has been working with Stones on their next album.

13 Fire at home of Mick Taylor and he and wife escape by means of an outside pipe.

15 Rory Gallagher says he has worked on Stones album. Robert Johnson, guitarist with Ox, joins the recording sessions in Amsterdam.

22 Talk of the Stones doing seven nights at New York's Madison Square Garden.

26 Harvey Mandel is rumoured as a replacement for Mick Taylor but this is denied.

MARCH

1 *The Rolling Stones*—film of Stones' concerts is said to have lost Dragon Aire Ltd around £1,000,000 ($2,000,000).

8 Stones win best-designed 'ad' award for Rock 'n' Roll by British pop paper, *New Musical Express*.

15 Mick and Marsha Hunt settle paternity suit out of court.

17 Soviet promoters say the Stones have lost their drive and that they are losing money at their Western concerts.

APRIL

14 Stones say Ron Wood will accompany them on their North and South American tour but it will be only a temporary arrangement.

MAY

1 Press gathering at New York's Fifth Avenue Hotel. Announcement made of Stones' three-month tour. Stones do an impromptu Lower Fifth Avenue concert from a flat-bed truck.

JUNE

1 The '75 tour of the Americas begins in Baton Rouge, Louisiana, at the Louisiana State University Assembly Center.

3 In San Antonio, Convention Center.

9-13 The Forum, Inglewood, Los Angeles.

15-16 Cow Palace, San Francisco.

17-18 In Toronto.

JULY

Issue in Britain by Decca of LP *Metamorphosis*.

AUGUST

2 US tour ends.

7-31 Stones tour Latin America, with concerts in Mexico City, Rio de Janeiro, São Paulo, and Venezuela.

SEPTEMBER

With several versions of 'Out Of Time' likely for UK chart position, Decca issue oldie version by the Stones of 'Out Of Time'.

NOVEMBER

Decca issue massive compilation of Stones tracks called *Rolled Gold* and it quickly makes the Top Ten.

DECEMBER

Rumours of a retirement concert by the Stones is denied. Mick and the Stones are recording their next album. Rumours circulate involving the Stones and Faces. Rod Stewart is announced as leaving the Faces because he learns Ron Wood will play on a Stones tour early in 1976. Mick denies Ron has joined the Stones. He says the group had hoped Ron Wood could join them for their tour, but that was all. At Christmas the issue becomes blurred.

1976

JANUARY

13 Sale held at Bonhams, Chelsea, of musical instruments and other items. Among those sold were an acoustic guitar belonging to Mick Taylor which fetched £60 ($120), a gold disc of *It's Only Rock 'n' Roll*, which made £78 ($158) and a fine lace shawl belonging to Bianca which fetched £22 ($45).

In New York Mick Jagger and Andy Warhol autograph Warhol prints of Jagger, 250 portfolios of ten prints. Each set is offered at £3,500 ($7,200), or individually at £425 ($875).

Mick Jagger commissions Warhol to paint four portraits of him.

Bianca Jagger abandons *Trick or Treat* film. She says some scenes were 'too dirty'.

Proposed British tour for spring cancelled.

Stones' next LP tentatively titled *Hot Stuff*.

FEBRUARY

12 Double album issued in Britain entitled *By Invitation Only*. The album contains Rolling Stones' 'It's Only Rock 'n' Roll'; it is compiled by British Radio 1 DJ Alan Freeman.

Above: Mick throws water over the audience during US tour. Left: The Stones give a free concert on New York's Fifth Avenue at the start of their tour. Below: The Stones' logo.

MEMBERS
of the
STONES

3
Mick Jagger

Mick has dominated the Stones in the media. Newspapers and magazines of all shades of opinion find constant titillation in his looks, purported statements, supposed actions. Fortunately the musical press has for the most part ignored Jagger the socialite, though at one time there was a deliberate editorial decision in certain quarters to avoid the more controversial Stones actions. This was done on the grounds that they were 'musical' papers and not gossip or general news publications.

The Mick Jagger of teen years, Kent-born in a middle-class family, once London University student, did have ambitions and this was to see himself among the big names of contemporary music. Jagger in no way saw himself as an industry pre-packaged pop star. He saw fame as something which comes through hard work and talent. He did regret leaving his academic life but the decision became necessary when there were obvious signs of the Stones being more than just another club group. And Jagger, like the others, enjoyed the acclaim and the fan worship, which was there from the beginning. Whatever may be said about some of his lyrics, attitudes and life style, it cannot be said that he ceased at any point to make music which mattered.

Jagger's close friends have always praised his originality, even if in the early days he and the Stones did exhibit a strange desire for comparison with the Beatles. Not a comparison in music but in style and success. And, when the Beatles disbanded, it was towards the Stones, Mick in particular, that the professional celebrity gossip columnists turned. The 'naughty' Mick became 'chic' and while film stars were ignored, reports and photos of Mick were wanted copy. Their day was made when Mick married Bianca and if copy wasn't about Bianca, her make-up, hair, looks and public appearances, then it was Mick and Bianca dining, filming, buying.

There were those foolish enough in the '60s who imagined that Mick was unintelligent because he looked rather unkempt, with straggling hair and bedraggled clothes. They mistook an image, nihilism à la Stones, for reality. Andrew Oldham, the Stones' manager, played the game well and the adult public savoured every morsel. They frothed and raged at the Stones with Mick the main target of their contempt at what this group supposedly stood for and the way in which it was influencing their precious offspring.

Author and journalist, James McMillan, in his book *The Roots of Corruption* (1972), talks of the hard-core hippies.

They regarded themselves as rebels who had rejected the standards and values of materialist civilization and this general attitude was reflected by the much more numerous pop groups and their dedicated fans.

In the public mind, the chief representative of this anti-convention movement, the very symbol of angry youth, using pop music as a medium of revolt was Michael Jagger.

Mick Jagger rode the newspaper chatter and public outcry with comparative indifference during the mid-late '60s. He never lost control even at times when the going became particularly hard, as for example when he and Keith faced possible imprisonment stemming from their arrests for supposedly possessing drugs. At this time it seemed that he was deliberately chosen as a victim by a British society looking for a scapegoat whose punishment and admonition would serve as an example of what could happen to any who followed in his wake.

Obviously Mick enjoyed some of this publicity or at least its positive repercussions, even if at times what was written wasn't too kind. Every artist and group needs constant exposure before a public which is faced with an endless choice of stars. As he once said, 'the media needs a story and the bands need to be publicized', and

sometimes for someone like Mick, the guy who had wanted since his teens to become a rock 'n' roll star, it can make people know you exist.

Flicking through the pages of Britain's musical paper *Record Mirror* through the years produces some interesting initial feature treatment on Mick. He was just one of the group during the flood of material from 1963 into 1964. He was pictured like the others looking at London Bridge, setting out with some trepidation and pride for America. The first solo Jagger picture seems to be in the issue dated 18 September 1964 though the copy itself did not single him out. The writer, not named, kept writing 'the boys' do this and that.

In the same issue a double-page spread of Stones pictures gave equal prominence to each member with no separate picture of Mick. However, he did occupy the centre of a group photo on 21 November and from then on he gradually moved towards becoming the group's leader. Mick talking with Roy Carr in *Creem* (July 1974) said:

I never really wanted to be the leader, but somehow I automatically got all the attention. I had the most recognizable features, etcetera, etcetera, etcetera, though I didn't really know or care. Brian cared a lot, but it didn't worry me.

That was the thing that messed Brian up—because he was desperate for attention. He wanted to be admired and loved and all that . . . which he was by a lot of people, but

it wasn't enough for him.

Chrissie Shrimpton had been working hard on Mick's lack of flamboyance from the moment they met and by 1967 *Record Mirror* could print a picture with the caption, 'Mick Jagger seen in front of his vast wardrobe, of many colourful clothes', and headline its copy, 'You Won't See Mick In Panto'.

In 1971 *Record Mirror* headlined, 'Could Jagger be Prime Minister?' This was Peter Jones, *RM*'s editor, being ingenious, for it was an analysis of M. Jagger who was born under the sign of Leo, with the generalization that many Leonians have become prime ministers. There was a grain of truth in the idea of Mick as Prime Minister, for he at one time had had keen political interests. He was a close friend of British MP Tom Driberg and it seems Driberg suggested on various occasions that Mick should become actively involved in the political scene.

Mick is well-read and interested in a wide range of subjects and indeed is far more lucid than some of his broadcast conversations have shown. However his political stance has puzzled various underground figures who would see him in the vanguard of their movement. During one of their American tours the Stones were visited by the political revolutionary, Abbie Hoffman. Mick was approached for financial aid in helping the trial of the Chicago Eight. He refused and said the Stones had their own trials. Hoffman later professed puzzlement as to where the Stones fit into the revolution.

With the media Jagger has often, one feels, been playing a game. At times he has deliberately adopted an articulate pose. This was shown on one major British TV interview where he was being given scant intellectual respect by the interviewer. Mick played the part well until perhaps he had the feeling, enough is enough, and instantly he became M. Jagger, university student, cold, analytical and rational. The interviewer gradually retreated and became a programme also-ran.

Mick Jagger's musical talent has been divided equally between Jagger the songwriter and Jagger the brilliant, extrovert, live performer, and in addition his recording activities with the Stones must not be forgotten.

His songwriting abilities soon became well known amongst people outside an immediate pop music circle and his early lyrics consistently made headlines. They belonged part and parcel to the mood and feelings of the time—at least the inward sentiments of some young people. Jagger criticized adults and he attacked conventional attitudes and behaviour customs prevalent in Britain.

More, his lyrics caught the boredom experienced by many young people who wanted to do things their way and were tired of paternal gifts from afar.

were pretty inoffensive, the Jagger words spelt conflict. While the Pete Townshend of 1965 was to be someone extolling 'my generation' and telling other people from other age groups, 'fade away', Mick Jagger was harshly and stridently vocalizing the complaint, 'I Can't Get No Satisfaction'. In another song he satirized mothers who took pills in an effort to get through their day. One commentator has described Jagger's caustic commentary as hypocritical, since many young people were into exactly the same game. However, he surely misses the point. The song, 'Mother's Little Helper', describes the antics of those who profess to being adult and to 'lead' and 'show' young people what is good living. The song suggests they do not know, any more than do some young people. The potent question becomes one of, 'Why do the adults who calmly escape via alcohol or pills from their problems attack young people for their habits?'

Obviously the Stones' songwriter was generalizing; not all adults by any means fall into this way of life, though his words have an increasing ring of truth as tranquillizers become acceptable to more and more people.

'Satisfaction' was THE song and almost the anthem for a permissive society where anything goes, although at the same time such a philosophy breeds its own innate boredom, its dissatisfaction and eventually becomes increasingly narcissistic and self-centred.

In America, the authorities changed 'Satisfaction's' second line, 'I Can't Get No Girlie Action', and the Stones changed 'Let's Spend The Night Together' to 'Let's Spend Some Time Together' to make the song palatable to American TV viewers. The song caused a great furore in Britain. It suggested you might sleep with your girlfriend, or at least people who pronounced on the subject said that this was what it meant. The Stones did not debate; they sang.

Mick's lyrics have also a strident note of masculine domination and there is more than an echo of cruelty and sadism. Much of this has been concealed from the average Stones listener by memorable tunes, as for instance in the songs, 'Brown Sugar', 'Under My Thumb' and 'Midnight Rambler'. How many swaying, excited dancers realize the full implication of these lyrics, even in the '70s with the supposed consciousness of women's lib and the retreat of male chauvinism? 'Brown Sugar' is white boy sexually triumphing over black girl in more ways than one. 'Under My Thumb' is just what it says, the girl who toes the line or enjoys being dominated. 'Midnight Rambler' is no mere Arnold Layne of Pink Floyd days, the one who collects women's apparel from clothes lines.

this one is a loose sexual marauder who doesn't ask. And there are other songs like 'Back Street Girl' and the memorable 'Star', which with clarity and perceptiveness describes the pop groupie.

The Stones were involved in drug culture and particularly so during the late '60s when acid-rock was in vogue and chemical substances highly exalted. Many of Mick's lyrics are concerned with this theme, though he was not in any way advocating drugs as a means towards higher consciousness. The major song is 'Sister Morphine'. And there are Mick's songs on *Their Satanic Majesties*; this was his and the group's musical offering during the bell and bead era.

Mick's lyrics from the time of 'Sympathy For The Devil' show an increasing preoccupation with the anti-Christ figure and among the Devil's achievements are several not at all incompatible with Mick's own wealth and taste.

Altamont brought the cold, sharp reality of the Devil, black magic world uncomfortably into focus, for there Mick's songs and vocalizing were no longer mere fun. For many, that day, the song was cold, stark reality.

Altamont in rock history stands as an apocalypse, where everything falls apart and society cannot cope with its own neuroses. A few of Mick's lyrics, such as 'Gimme Shelter', continue the general feeling of hopelessness. 'Street Fighting Man' has always been seen as a classic Jagger song but, as one of the few socio-political numbers, it does not make any more than a surface analysis of the forces directing so much of our lives. In fact the lyric suggests non-involvement with 'But what can a poor boy do except to sing for a rock 'n' roll band?' Such a line has been conveniently forgotten by those in America who have seen the song as a strident anthem of the alternative society, the street marchers.

Mick of *Goat's Head Soup* era has, it seems, let lyrics waste and the same goes for *Exile On Main Street*, though on the latter there is the theme of growing old with the music as instanced in 'Soul Survivor' and 'Torn And Frayed'. The old themes do intrude along the way and as American writer, Robert Christagau, has said, they are of 'sex as power, sex as love, sex as pleasure, distance, craziness, release'. Whether in the future music will totally dominate Stones songs remains for future commentary. Perhaps Mick Jagger has lost his anger and has like many rock lyricists become settled into a philosophy which advocates living for oneself in one's own way and to hell with society. That may or may not be true.

As a stage performer, Mick Jagger has few competitors in the greatest live vocalist stakes. Even in his 30s he has a commanding and electrifying

presence and a general movement more befitting a younger person.

His gestures and stylized movements blend admirably with lyrics and music. He has something of the clown in his exaggerated gestures and expressions. He teases and titillates and is blessed with an admirable saucy, sexy mouth. Among the general rock vocalists who merely produce as far as possible their own and their group's recorded sound, Jagger stands out as a masterful figure. He knows the essence of the real live vocalist-actor.

Perpetually, music press writers and others ask how long Mick will continue. Who knows? Does he?

Above: Mick in characteristic action. Right: The most expressive and most photographed face in rock's history, whether male or female; a mixture of the gentle, ugly, tough, defiant, abrasive, aggressive, painful. There are camp gestures, pouting lips and, amidst the almost satanic leers, hints of tenderness and generosity for friend and foe. No *one* face is his

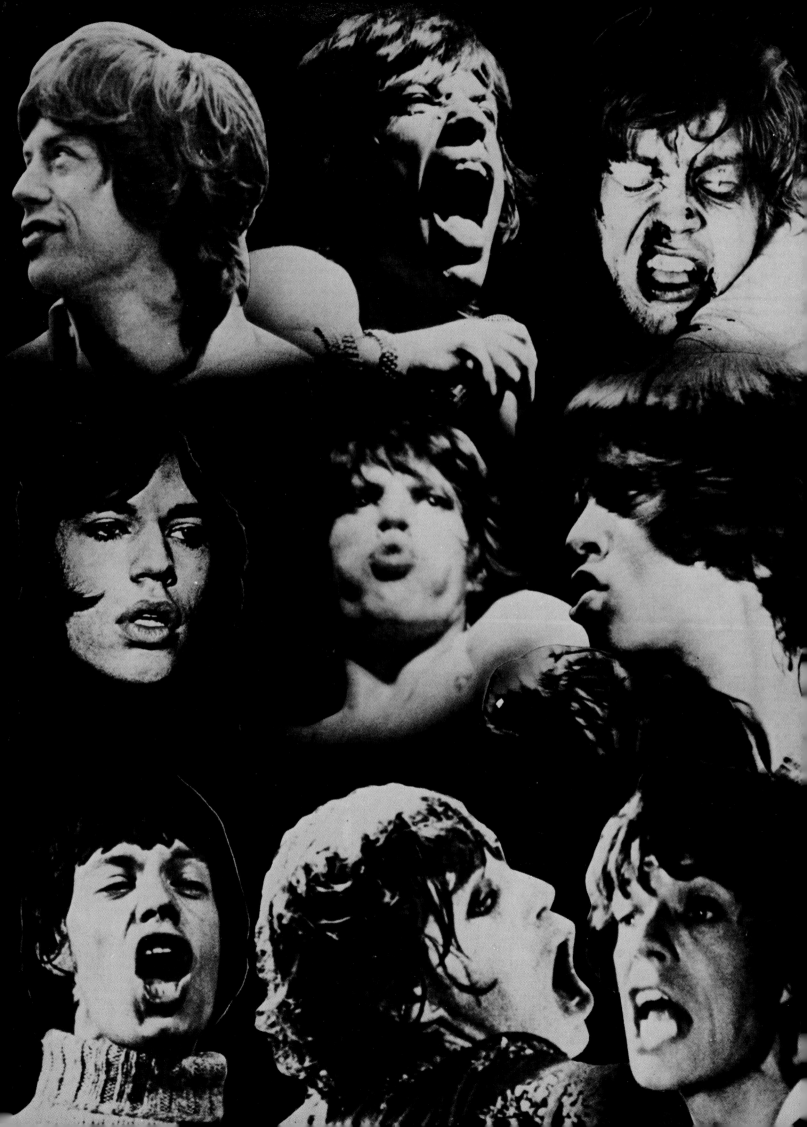

Keith Richard

Keith grew up with Mick, though their association in pre- and early teen years was rather limited. Both lived in Dartford, Kent, and their parents resided in the same block. They both went to junior school at the age of seven. Mick says, 'We knew each other . . . we weren't great friends.'

In those days in Britain, the '50s, most people attending day schools divided themselves into two groups at the age of eleven or twelve. One group, the minority, were sent to grammar school, and the other to the secondary modern. Mick went to the local grammar school but Keith went to the other school. This inevitably widened the gulf between the two.

Mick comments: 'I used to see Keith riding to school on his bike. Then I saw him again when he used to catch the train to get to school and I was on the same train to attend college.' This was when Mick was about seventeen. The meeting proved an eventful one. They both loved music and had in common with any British teenager into music a craving for Americana. Everything good, then, came from the States, whether bubble-gum or Elvis and for the more sophistic-ated, Muddy Waters. Black music had little radio airing apart from someone like the DJ Tony Hall. Hall spun London-American platters plus releases on Brunswick. He was one of the few chinks of musical light for people like Mick and Keith.

The result of their renewed ac-quaintance led to musical practice times on guitar and some avid record listening. Eventually of course both met Brian at the Bricklayers' Arms and heard him at the Ealing Club and they set up flat together to pursue their musical love and ambitions.

Even in those days, Keith was very much in the background. Mick's frequent singing forays at the Ealing Club saw Keith sitting things out. His kind of sound wasn't wanted by the more blues-orientated organizers and audiences. Unknown to anyone, he and the others were busily practising and rehearsing a sound which would prove a riotous success once they played the clubs and established a residency at the Crawdaddy Club, at the Station Hotel in Richmond.

Keith Richard has had very little press over the years. He gives few interviews and is obviously totally unconcerned. Like the others he has been willing to allow Mick the lime-light, though stage-wise both are extrovert. Yet his work as a musician is most important within the general Stones sound and his forte has been

in songwriting in collaboration with Mick.

Initially, both were somewhat diffident about their writing talents. Their early discs, like those of the Beatles, contained dollops of American material. Their early releases were of this kind: 'Not Fade Away' was an old Buddy Holly—Crickets number; Willie Dixon wrote 'Little Red Rooster', and 'Come On' was a Chuck Berry track. And their first Top Twenty record, 'I Wanna Be Your Man', came from the Beatles, a pretty straightforward song if ever there was one and only made palatable by it suiting the frenetic energy of the Stones.

And on stage the Stones played popular ballroom numbers like 'Poison Ivy' and 'I Can Tell'. 'Come On' never

impressed the Stones. It took ages being recorded and, in spite of their opinion of it, it did make its mark around the ballrooms where the Stones played. At the same time it gave them ideas of writing their own material.

Keith is the musician in the Jagger —Richard songwriting team. Together they've written most of the Stones hits apart from during the early years and some material included on albums released on their own label in the '70s.

There has been considerable variation in their songs as is seen, for instance, in a comparison of 'Sympathy For The Devil' with 'As Tears Go By'. They can be both loud and raucous and touchingly simple.

Keith and Mick have through the years provided songs for a number of people. Marianne Faithfull had a big hit with 'As Tears Go By'; Cliff Richard recorded 'Blue Turns To Grey'; there was a massive hit for Gene Pitney and 'That Girl Belongs To Yesterday'; while Chris Farlowe had a big UK smash with 'Out Of Time'. A short-lived team called Twice As Much did well with 'Sittin' On A Fence' and 'Satisfaction' has been recorded by many including Wilson Pickett and Aretha Franklin.

Mick talked with journalist-author Roy Carr for the American magazine, *Creem*, in July 1974 and, discussing the role Keith played in their musical writing partnership, said:

> Keith used to write all the music and a lot of times he'd give me the title or mood of a song. Like 'Gimme Shelter'. He'd play the music and say something like Gimme Shelter and I'd go on from there. I still do this with a lot of Keith's songs.

However, at other times, they wrote together and Mick is particularly pleased with one song coming from this process, 'Time Waits For No One'. One other permutation was also favoured. Each would write independently and then leave the other to fill in the gaps or fill out the material suggested.

In many instances the band itself as a team would contribute towards arrangement. Keith told author George Tremlett:

> Our music is drawn from the influences of white and Negro folk music. We try to reflect forward-looking attitudes. You have to be progressive when you write for young people.

Keith still has an affection for early Stones material, particularly the Chuck Berry repertoire, even though Mick rather ignores it now, as if the past is now no longer of concern. In early days Keith also admired the Beatles, though this was common to the group for, as Mick says, 'I think everyone got turned on the idea of writing by the Beatles. It was like "If the Beatles can write, we can write".'

And Keith the guitarist? His forte

Left: Keith Richard playing on British T.V. Programme, Thank Your Lucky Stars, early in the Stones' career. Above: Keith and Anita Pallenberg – desperate reaction to the fire at their home.

may be songwriting but he is hardly less distinguished in his guitar-playing. He provides a dominating backing to the group, and it is he who directs rehearsals and dictates the musical spectrum. He provides consummate musical wrappings, along with the others, for the Jagger vocal extravaganzas and cover for Mick's stage-circuit training.

He remains hidden for the most part from journalists, writers and visual media personnel and once he said, 'The writers from the rock press are so deadly serious. They treat me as if I were Stravinsky. It's absurd.'

One facet of Keith's life, however, besides the occasional references to him and Anita, has interested the gossip columnists, and that is his teeth. They have been described as pretty bad through the years and news during the '70s of his making for dentistry circles caused an amazing ripple in the press. It is a pity perhaps that such a trivial matter has exercised the pens of people who could be describing Keith Richard, the songwriter and musician.

Brian Jones

Mick and Keith heard and met Brian Jones for the first time at the Ealing Club. Their mutual love for blues and doubtless stories of past skiffle memories welded them together into a trio determined to become experts in the music they loved, an interest which seemingly few shared at the time. So they shared a flat together and practised their music.

The story of Brian Jones of course goes further back. He grew up in a working-class family in Cheltenham and went to the boys' grammar school which was conveniently situated next to the girls'. Brian was known as 'Buster' among other names. He played washboard in a local skiffle group when he was about fourteen or fifteen.

Chris Rowe was often the group's singer and she remembers Brian's frequent losing of the vital thimble. They practised in the Community Centre, Rowanfield Estate, or at people's houses.

Chris remembers his beautiful blond hair. He, like others, sometimes found Cheltenham rather dead and certainly in those days seemingly miles from London. The British capital city seemed part of another country.

She says, 'We were just kids messing about. There was no long-term planning. We did things on the spur of the moment.'

When the skiffle band folded, most of the group joined the Chet Valley Jazz Men. Brian didn't. In spite of a very good school record he drifted from job to job and at the same time

Below: The Brian who often wandered into his own world. Above right: At peace, and reflective.

got interested in what he once described as 'drinks, girls and things'.

He left home and established his own flat in Cheltenham before he finally took the road to London. Alexis Korner's Band had played at Cheltenham and Brian introduced himself after the concert. Alexis gave him his London address and telephone number.

Then followed the meeting with Mick and Keith and eventually the formation of the Rolling Stones, their first disc and tour. In those early Stones days Brian was certainly the most hospitable and the best dressed of them all. On stage he attracted as many, if not more, girls than Mick. Yet he had a basic insecurity which never allowed him to fall in with anything for too long. Change was the operative word.

Close associates describe Brian as someone who was very tender but 'a mixed-up feller'. He was very intelligent, often charming and good company. Yet he would get himself into hassles and be his own worst enemy. They say, 'He was more sinned against than sinning.'

According to some writers he and Mick had a personality clash and Brian was accordingly gradually played out of the Stones. Others would say not. They would point to Brian's own identity problems which could not coexist in a musically determined group like the Stones. They could not afford to carry someone who was weak if real success in the pop world was at all possible.

Others have described lurid stories of the Jagger-Jones relationship, including that of a rather bizarre knife fight at Brian's house. Mick Jagger calls this story ridiculous and so does Bill Wyman. Mick has said that it was the invention of Marianne Faithfull who talked to Anthony Scaduto for his book on Mick. Mick did not talk to the author. He has said: 'She just made up those stories and anyone who knows Marianne . . . even this guy Scaduto knows that she made most of it up.'

One other major incident in the Brian Jones—Stones story surrounds his love for Anita Pallenberg. He met her through various youthful members of the aristocracy in London who found the Stones 'chic'. Some say she exercised a bad influence over him and was responsible for some of his weird acts such as dressing up in a Nazi uniform with his foot upon a Jewish-looking person. Not surprisingly the bad taste of this event brought condemnation from many sources and it gave the Stones as a group a bad name. Most people say Brian loved her deeply but Keith also admired and loved her and eventually she left Brian for Keith.

Brian's death will always be shrouded in mystery but most people intimate with the Stones find 'suicide' the least likely explanation. The official coroner's verdict was accidental death, though popular chatter has tended to dramatize the affair.

Musically, Brian became less and

less influential as the period of *Their Satanic Majesties* approached. David Dalton sums it up well in his *Rolling Stones* when he writes:

Perhaps his most effective influence was in the middle period in songs like 'Paint It Black' and '19th Nervous Breakdown' where his buzzing, demon-like sitar changed the axis of the songs so that they took on a strange, plaintive, menacing tone.

Dalton remarks on Brian's playing of the dulcimer in 'Lady Jane' and flute in 'Ruby Tuesday'. There was in his playing delicious simplicity with the right degree of sensitivity.

Brian never made a solo album, the nearest being his recording of music found in North Africa. He spent one night at Jajouka and then for weeks afterwards experimented and played with the music and its taping, running it backwards and overlaying it upon itself. It obviously fascinated him. The record was released by Rolling Stones Records after his death.

Whatever may or may not be said about Brian Jones, from a purely musical point of view his death was a waste, though who knows what his future would have been if he had not drowned. Life had certainly become very sour.

Right: A strident musical Brian wrapped up in his playing. Below: Brian with Anita Pallenberg. Later she became Keith's girlfriend.

Bill Wyman

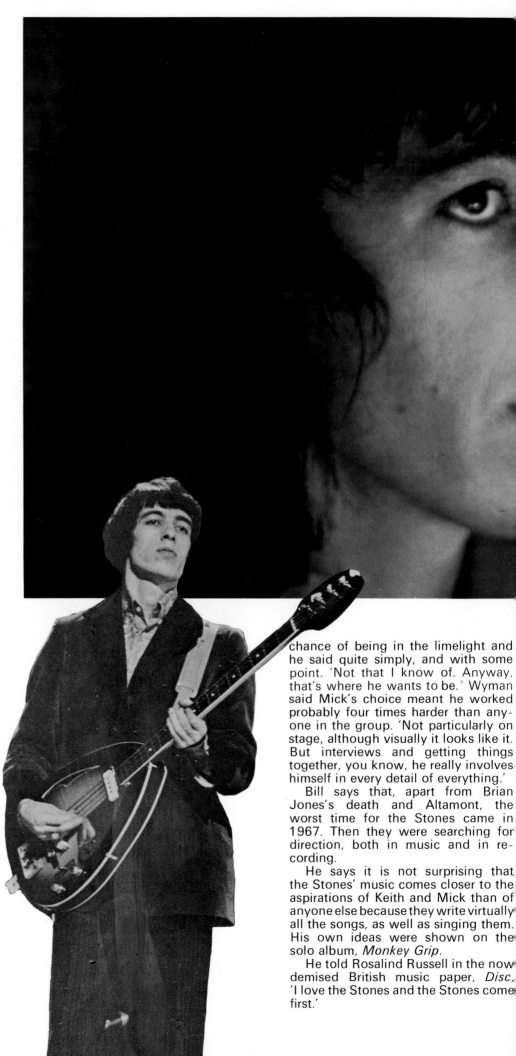

Bill Wyman has always been called the 'quiet Stone'. His father was a bricklayer and Bill attended Oakfield Junior School in Penge, Kent, and then Beckenham Grammar School. He was employed as a bookmaker's clerk in London before joining the Royal Air Force. After this he worked for a time with an engineering firm in south London. He was the last person to join the first complete Stones' personnel set-up. He was playing for a local Penge rock 'n' roll group when he saw an advertisement for a bass player. The group was the Stones and Bill played several practice sessions with them. In describing these, he told Richard Green of the *New Musical Express* (May 1964):

> . . . they didn't like me, but I had a good amplifier, and they were badly in need of amplifiers at that time! So they kept me on. Later, when they were going to get rid of me, I think I clicked or something, and I stayed. I must have fitted in.

Bill is the oldest member of the Stones. Born 24 October 1936 he was one of five children. His interests outside the Stones have been varied. He is a keen student of astronomy and a good photographer. He has a fan's fanaticism for blues records, though his collection, which is considerable, covers many early styles of music. He owned a large house near Beckenham and had his own studio there but when he parted from his wife, Diane, he acquired his dream home, Gedding Hall, a Suffolk mansion built mainly during the reign of Henry VIII. In 1974 he rented property near Venice for himself and girlfriend, Astrid Lundström.

By the end of 1975 he had issued two solo singles, 'White Lightning' and 'Monkey Grip Glue', and an album, *Monkey Grip*. He was joined in his album recording by Dr John and Leon Russell. Bill became interested in a group called Tucky Buzzard and produced their first album called *She's A Striker*.

He believes the Stones have continued as a recording and live group because of their ability to create, within the limitations imposed from without, both a private and rock star life. He told reporter Peter Harvey:

> A lot of groups live together practically, you know what I mean. We just split to various parts of the world when we are not working. And then when we get back together again it's good fun. 'How are you? How you been for the past couple of months?'

Peter Harvey asked him whether he felt Mick Jagger had lessened his own chance of being in the limelight and he said quite simply, and with some point. 'Not that I know of. Anyway, that's where he wants to be.' Wyman said Mick's choice meant he worked probably four times harder than anyone in the group. 'Not particularly on stage, although visually it looks like it. But interviews and getting things together, you know, he really involves himself in every detail of everything.'

Bill says that, apart from Brian Jones's death and Altamont, the worst time for the Stones came in 1967. Then they were searching for direction, both in music and in recording.

He says it is not surprising that the Stones' music comes closer to the aspirations of Keith and Mick than of anyone else because they write virtually all the songs, as well as singing them. His own ideas were shown on the solo album, *Monkey Grip*.

He told Rosalind Russell in the now demised British music paper, *Disc*, 'I love the Stones and the Stones come first.'

Charlie Watts

Les Perrin describes Charlie Watts as 'very together', and writer George Tremlett says he could well be the happiest member of the group. Charlie Watts is the Stones' drummer. He was born in 1941 and brought up in north London not far from the famous Wembley stadium and Empire Pool, home of some dramatic and memorable Stones concerts.

Charlie is further described by Les Perrin as 'well adjusted' and he refers with approval to the private life of the Stones' drummer. His wife Shirley is a sculptor. Les talks of their interest in a world he himself enjoys, that of sheepdogs, and notes with fond approval that Shirley was Charlie's successor to the Presidency of the North

Wales Sheepdog Society in 1976.

He describes Charlie Watts as a quiet man, the sort of person who considers carefully what he says. Watts has said, 'I'm basically lazy . . . I've never found something I really wanted to do outside the Stones.'

Yet, as Les Perrin says, he has his Welsh ponies and sheepdogs and to these can be added an interest in antique furniture and in various historical periods like that of Victoria and the American Civil War. He has considerable interest in jazz and indeed wrote and illustrated a book, *Ode to a High-Flying Bird*, about Charlie Parker, the famous American jazz player.

As a drummer, Charlie says he is very much an 'on-off' man and thus tomorrow might be a good night and the next, not. He once told writer, Lon Goddard, 'I take one step at a time and forget each afterwards. You don't forget what you've learnt, but you dissociate yourself from doing anything near the same again and try a totally new vein.'

Like Bill Wyman, Charlie has never been involved in the various scandals, particularly those involving drugs, which have hit the Stones from time to time and it's very possible that while most members of the public know Mick Jagger few, if any, know the name of Charlie Watts. He is admired by musical fans of the Stones for his rhythms underlying the group's sound and for the sensitive mood and feel he has for what is happening around him.

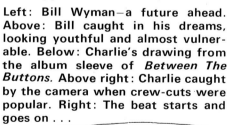

Left: Bill Wyman—a future ahead. Above: Bill caught in his dreams, looking youthful and almost vulnerable. Below: Charlie's drawing from the album sleeve of *Between The Buttons*. Above right: Charlie caught by the camera when crew-cuts were popular. Right: The beat starts and goes on . . .

Ian Stewart

Ian Stewart, once described as 'the stone that rolled away', has for many years lurked in the background. He was associated with the Stones right from the start. Along with Dick Taylor, Keith, Mick and Brian he could be found rehearsing music at the Bricklayers' Arms. Even when Dick Taylor had left and Bill Wyman and Charlie Watts had come onto the scene, Ian Stewart remained. In the end, however, he chose job security and kept his employment with ICI in London.

Later he became road manager for the Stones and has at times played piano and organ at gigs. He is also credited on various Stones recordings. He was on 'Come On' but much more in the fore on 'Stoned', the B side of 'I Wanna Be Your Man'.

In an interview with Peter Jones for *Record Mirror* (23 September 1973) he talked of the aggro the Stones have faced as a group and if people saw money and luxury surrounding the group, then he suggested they saw what they wanted to see. He talked of insults and worse faced by the five. He was not denying that money had come in later days, but stressing that it was money at a price.

Ian Stewart. He began with the boys when they dreamt of stardom.

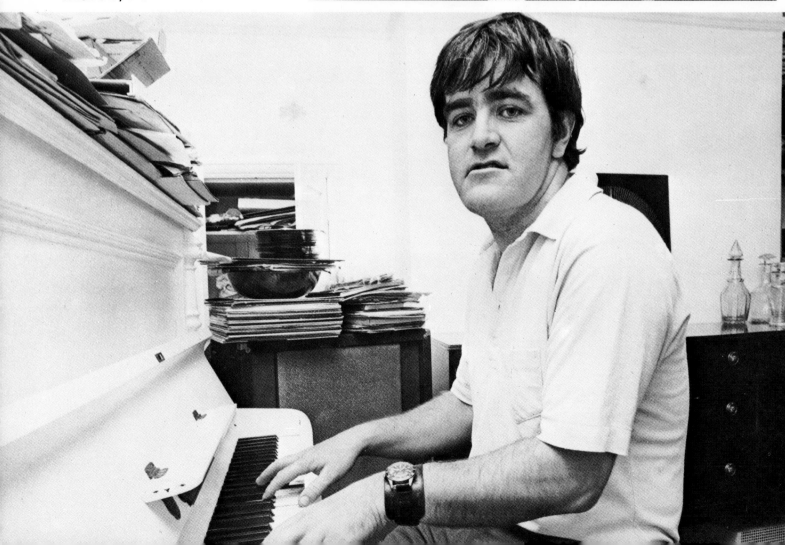

Mick Taylor

Mick Taylor joined the Rolling Stones on 8 June 1969 and left the group on 14 December 1974 to pursue his own musical ideas. Hence Taylor, who replaced the ailing Brian Jones, was immediately thrown into the US tour of 1969 and in the following year, that of Europe. Mick Taylor always kept a low profile in the group. The various press releases for the Stones' tours usually content themselves with saying his father was an aircraft worker and that he attended Onslow Secondary School, Hatfield, England. He spent several months as an artist engraver. Taylor was 22 when he joined the Stones and had been a member of the famous and influential John Mayall Blues Breakers, which had produced such great guitarists as Eric Clapton and Jimmy Page. Taylor at the time of his press conference on 13 July 1969

said he had never met the group and his first contact with them came when Mick Jagger phoned him and asked whether he was interested in joining the Stones. Taylor said, however, that he had always followed the group and been fascinated by their sound.

His time with the Stones was short; a little over five years. It did mean he filled the musical gap left by Brian Jones. It also meant the Stones were enabled musically to find a togetherness which they had been losing during Brian's trials and tribulations. Mick Taylor toured the States with the group but found his admiration of the group lessened when he became personally involved in their musical effotts. So he left to pursue his own musical freedom.

Mick Taylor, the musician. He never really seemed keen on the extrovert activities of other members of the band.

Ron Wood

Ron Wood has had a chequered musical history. He played with the Stones on their 1975 American tour. His playing with Eric Clapton at London's Rainbow (which is now closed) in January 1973 really highlighted his talent and this was confirmed in his first solo album which was issued in 1974 under the title of *I Have My Own Album To Do*.

His solo work featured many of the best rock musicians and saw Wood's first contact with the Stones. For example, Keith Richard had called in at the recording sessions and ended up by more or less staying for a few weeks, doing overdubs, basic tracks, vocals and offering a few songs.

With the album's completion, Ron Wood felt he would enjoy taking his session band on stage and so two sold-out concerts were held. The band comprised Keith, Andy Newmark (Sly Stone) on drums, Willie Weeks, bass, and Ian McLagan on keyboards.

Wood was a founding member of the Jeff Beck group and has become a permanent fixture with the Faces. His presence with the Stones in their 1975 America tour was simply as a guest appearance.

Billy Preston

Billy Preston, born in Houston but Los Angeles bred, began playing music in church and has worked with famous names like Mahalia Jackson and James Cleveland. In 1962 he joined Sam Cooke and Little Richard for a somewhat hectic and well-received tour. At its end, Billy recorded *Sixteen-Year-Old-Soul*, an album for Cooke's Star label.

Preston was heard by famous singer Ray Charles and invited to record for Vee Jay. The result was a duo album with Ray Charles entitled *The Most Exciting Organ Ever*. A single from the album, 'Billy's Bag', gained him inter-

Ron Wood, a constant 'occasional' group member.

Billy Preston featured on '75 US tours.

est in Britain and during 1967–8 he toured Europe.

His major European breakthrough came when Paul McCartney invited him to join the Beatles on the single 'Get Back'. It worked so well that Billy Preston stayed around and played electric piano on all the *Let It Be* sessions. He cut two albums for the Beatles' Apple label, *That's The Way God Planned It* and *Encouraging Words*, both co-produced by George Harrison. When he left Apple he signed with A&M Records and there made four albums and several successful US singles, 'Will It Go Round In Circles', 'Space Race', and 'Nothing From Nothing'.

Preston toured the States with the Stones in 1972 and accepted a further invitation for the '75 tour.

Ollie Brown

Ollie Brown was the percussionist on the '75 Rolling Stones tour of the Americas and has spent most of the '70s as one of the most in-demand record sessionmen in Hollywood.

His career began in Detroit while still at high school and he gained national acclaim for his work in the Stevie Wonder Band which accompanied the Stones on their 1972 tour of the States.

Brown continued his work with Stevie after that tour and has been involved with Stevie's recording of his wife, Syreeta. He has also worked with Billy Preston and a string of top name artists like Barbra Streisand, Joe Cocker, The Temptations and Spinners.

Ollie Brown, Billy Preston and members of the Stones.

nd

65

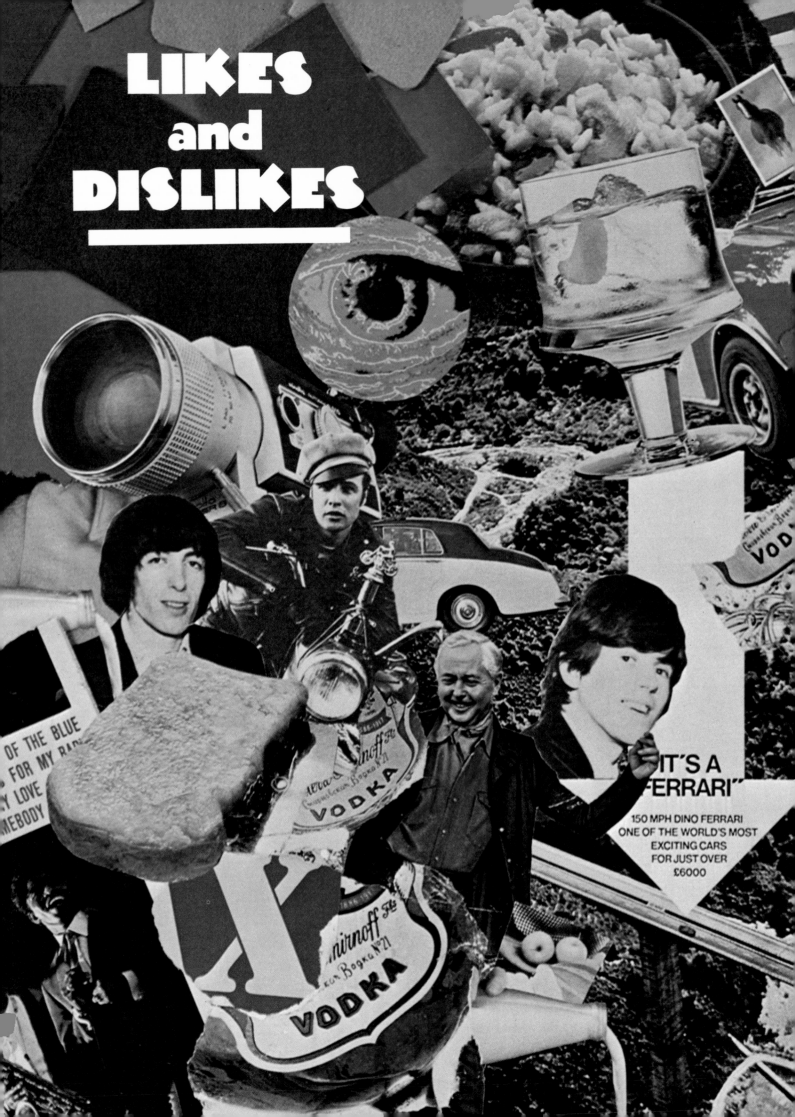

LIKES
and
DISLIKES

Once the Stones featured in many 'teen' magazines and were consequently asked about their favourite drink, clothes, likes and dislikes. For those Rolling Stones veteran fans with a liking for nostalgia here is one of their early question profiles, made available through the kindness of the long-standing and respected Stones publicist, Les Perrin.

Posing for a Stones jigsaw perhaps or just a pile of Stones? Short-haired, suited, and unsophisticated.

Age entered show business: 21
First public appearance: Marquee, London
First professional appearance: Crawdaddy, Richmond, Surrey
Biggest break in career: Ian Stewart
Biggest disappointment in career: Meeting Charlie Watts
TV debut: Thank Your Lucky Stars
Radio debut: Saturday Club
Biggest influence on career: Chuck Berry
Former occupation before show business: Clerical and engineering
Hobbies: Tape-recording and home movies
Favourite colour: Blue
Favourite food: Cheese on toast and veal
Favourite drink: Milk
Favourite clothes: Casual
Favourite singer: Mose Allison
First important public appearance: The Royal Albert Hall
Favourite actor/actress: Marlon Brando, Charlie Watts
Favourite band/instrumentalist: James Brown
Favourite groups: Spencer Davis
Favourite composer: Cole Porter
Miscellaneous likes: Young ladies, cashew nuts, R & B, tape-recorders, chewing gum
Miscellaneous dislikes: Marmalade, Jonathan King, arguments
Best friend: Nobody
Most thrilling experience: Playing live shows
Tastes in music: All good music
Pets: Dog—Shetland collie called Lucky
Personal ambition: See the world
Professional ambition: Be a millionaire

Biggest break in career: Meeting Bill Wyman
Biggest disappointment in career: Meeting Charlie Watts
TV debut: Thank Your Lucky Stars
Radio debut: Saturday Club
Own TV or Radio Series: They won't give us one
Biggest influence on career: The soul of J. S. Bach
Former occupations before show business: Tram driver in Istanbul
Hobbies: Biting my nails
Favourite colour: Black
Favourite food: Apples
Favourite drink: Vodka
Favourite clothes: Mine
Favourite singer: Elton Hayes
First important public appearance: Pop Prom Albert Hall
Favourite actor/actress: Harold Wilson
Favourite bands/instrumentalists: Victor Sylvester
Favourite groups: None
Favourite composers: Lennon/McCartney, J. S. Bach, Carole King
Car: Bentley
Miscellaneous dislikes: Headaches, corns, pimples, gangrene
Best friend: Mick Jagger and Charlie Watts
Most thrilling experience: Dying
Tastes in music: Blues to Baroque missing out Dean Martin
Pets: Ratbag—a dog, I think
Personal ambition: To go to Church
Professional ambition: To make a good film
Forthcoming disc (or film) projects: Yes

Real name: Bill Wyman
Professional name: The Rolling Stones
Birthdate: 24 October 1941
Birthplace: Lewisham
Personal points: Height, 5ft 8in; Weight, 119lbs
Colour of eyes: Green
Colour of hair: Black
Parents' names: William and Kathleen
Brothers' and sisters' names: John, Judy, Ann, Paul
Wife's name: Diane
Children: Stephen
Present house: Farnborough, Kent
Instruments played: Bass, piano
Where educated: Beckenham Grammar School
Musical education: Piano lessons for three years from age of ten

Real name: Keith Richards
Professional name: Valerie Masters
Birthdate: 18 December 1944
Birthplace: Dartford, Kent
Personal points: Height, 5ft 10in; Weight, Don't know
Colour of eyes: Red
Colour of hair: Brown
Parents' names: Boris and Dirt (or Doris and Bert)
Brothers' and sisters' names: As far as known—none
Husband and wife's name: Ditto
Children: Ditto
Present house: None of your business
Instruments played: Guitar
Where educated: Dr Barnardo's
Musical education: As far as known—none
Age entered show business: 18 years old
First public appearance as amateur: Eltham, 1959
First professional appearance: Marquee in 1962

Real name: Michael P. Jagger
Professional name: Vince Whirlwind
Birthdate: 26 July 1944
Birthplace: Dartford, Kent
Personal points: Height, 5ft 10in; Weight: Don't know
Colour of eyes: Blue
Colour of hair: Brown
Parents' names: Joe and Eva
Brothers' and sisters' names: Chris
Husband and wife's name:
Present home: Golders Green
Instruments played: Harmonica
Where educated: Dartford Grammar School and London School of Economics
Musical education: None
Age entered show business: Ask Andrew—19 I think
First public appearance as an amateur: Harrow Youth Centre
First professional appearance: Marquee
Biggest disappointment in career: Not meeting Elvis
TV debut: Thank Your Lucky Stars
Radio debut: Saturday Club

Own TV or Radio Series: Mark Time
in 1957
Biggest influence on career: I
honestly can't think
Former occupation before show
business: Student
Hobbies: Photography, houses,
horses, birds
Favourite colours: Red, blue,
yellow, green, pink, black, white
Favourite food: Very highly
flavoured nosh—Continental
Favourite drink: Vodka and orange
and lemon juice
Favourite clothes: My father's
Favourite singers: Otis Redding,
James Brown, Herman Munster,
Beatles, Bill Wyman, Wilson Pickett
First important public appearance:
Albert Hall
Favourite actor/actress: Michael
Caine and Steve McQueen
Favourite groups: Beatles, Who,
Hank B. Marvin
Favourite composers; Lennon &
McCartney, McCormick/Place,
Keith, Otis Redding
Car: Mini-Cooper
Miscellaneous likes: Beans, new
things, cars, dogs, finishing new
records
Miscellaneous dislikes: Tomatoes,
rude Americans
Best friend: David Bailey
Most thrilling experience: First
time we made a record
Tastes in music: R & B, pop etc.
Pets: Dog—Theodora
Personal ambition: To be happy
Professional ambition: To make a
film before I die
Name of accompanists: Keith, Brian,
Bill and Charlie—the fab fellas
Major awards: All sorts of petrol
companies which Brian's got
Compositions: 'Blue Turns To Grey';
'It Should Be You'; for 'George
Bean' and others ask for list
Origin of stage name: Our heads
Film appearances: Dirty documentaries

Real name: Charles
Robert Watts
Professional name:
The Rolling Stones
Birthdate: 2 June 1942
Birthplace: Islington
Personal points: Height, 5ft 9in;
Weight, 143lbs
Colour of eyes: Blue
Colour of hair: Brown
Parents' names: Charles and Lily
Brothers' and sisters' names: Linda
Husband and wife's name: Shirley
Children:
Present home: Near Brighton, Sussex
Instruments played: Drums
Where educated: Tylers Croft School
Musical education: None
Age entered show business: Can't
remember

First public appearance as an amateur:
Can't remember
First professional appearance: With
Alexis Korner
Biggest break in career: Don't know
Biggest disappointment in career:
Don't know
TV debut: Lucky Stars
Radio debut: Saturday Club
Former occupations before show
business: Commercial artist
Hobbies: Collecting antique firearms,
modelling in plaster
Favourite colours: Red, blue and
black
Favourite food: Don't know
Favourite drink: Tea
Favourite clothes: Any
Favourite singer: Haven't got one
First important public appearance:
Haven't got one
Favourite actor/actress: Haven't
got one
Favourite bands/instrumentalist:
Don't know
Favourite group: Beatles
Favourite composers: Cole Porter,
Lenon & McCartney,
Duke Ellington
Miscellaneous likes: Jazz
Miscellaneous dislikes: Working
Best friend: Haven't got one
Most thrilling experience: Don't
know
Tastes in music: Any sort
Pets: Pony, cat and collie dog
Personal ambition: Haven't got one
Professional ambition: Haven't got
one

Real name:
Brian Jones
Professional name:
The Rolling Stones
Birthdate: 28 February 1944
Birthplace: Cheltenham,
Gloucestershire
Personal points: Height, 5ft 8in;
Weight, 130lbs
Colour of eyes: Greeny/Grey
Colour of hair: Blond
Parents' names: Lewis and Louisa
Brothers' and sisters' names: Husband
Stew and he works at glass furnace
Present home: Chelsea
Instruments played: Guitar,
harmonicas, piano, organ, autoharp,
koto, clarinet, sax
Where educated: School
Musical education: Copying Negro-
blues records
Age entered show business: Four
months
First public appearance as amateur:
Baby show at West Gloucestershire
Women's Institute Annual Show
First professional appearance:
Marquee, 1962
Biggest break of career: Break with
parents

Biggest disappointment in career:
Never been to Korea
TV debut: Crowd artist/TV, News 195?
Radio debut: Choir boy Sunday Half
Hour 195?
Own TV or radio series: Children's
TV programme called All My Sons
Biggest influence on career:
British press
Former occupation before show
business: Various and nondescript
Hobbies: Collecting obscure musical
instruments, photography
Favourite colour: Brown, green,
black, white
Favourite food: Steaks, English
home cooking
Favourite drink: Ice-cold lager
Favourite clothes: Summer: light
clothes; Winter: olde Englishe
tweed
Favourite singer: Otis Redding,
Wilson Pickett, Steve Winwood
First public appearance: The
Marquee, London
Favourite bands/instrumentalists:
Booker T and The M.G.'s
Favourite group: Spencer Davis
Favourite composers: Lennon &
McCartney
Car: Have a Rolls Royce; would
like an Automobil Tornada and Mini
Miscellaneous likes: Girls, Y-fronts
Miscellaneous dislikes: Liver,
ignorant reporters, people who
ask what I think about the Beatles
getting their MBEs
Best friend: A number of
acquaintances
Most thrilling experience: Read
about it in the *News of the World*
(note: a somewhat 'spicy'.
'investigative' British Sunday
newspaper)
Tastes in music: Catholic
Pets:
Personal ambition: To be happy in
everything
Professional ambition: I hope things
carry on as they are

For car fans the following publicity
note was given out in the '70s
ROLLING STONES' AUTOMOBILES

Mick Jagger:
Mercedes 6.3—300 SEL in Gold
Ferrari Daytona in Silver Grey
Renault 16 in Blue
Cadillac (1934) in Grey
Two motorbikes—BSA and Honda
Keith Richard:
Ferrari Dino in Silver Grey
Jaguar E-type in Red
Pontiac (1950) in Black
"Maigret" Renault
Bill Wyman:
Citroën Maserati
Charlie Watts:
Citroën Maserati; Mercedes

A-Z of
PERSONALITIES

AN A TO Z OF THE PEOPLE WHO MET THE STONES ALONG THE WAY

Arnold, Shirley: Once, and a long-serving, director of the Stones' fan club.

Baud, Lucien Abbé: Pastor of the Fisherman's Chapel of St Anne, St Tropez, priest who married Mick and Bianca.

Bergman, Jo: Familiar face around the rock camps and traveller with the Stones for five years and involved at times with tour organization.

Bianca: See section two of this volume and 'Mick Jagger'.

Block, Judge: The British Justice, who sentenced Mick and Keith for periods of imprisonment.

Brise, Sir John Ruggle: Lord-Lieutenant of Essex on whose country estate took place a famous British TV discussion between Mick Jagger and notables.

Bulgakov, Mikhail: Russian author of *The Master and Margarita*, a book introduced to Mick by Marianne Faithfull, from whence came the theme for the famous Stones song, 'Sympathy For The Devil'.

Cammell, Donald: He persuaded Mick Jagger to play in the film, *Performance*.

Chess, Marshall: He became head of the Rolling Stones record company and was a notable record company figure.

Clapton, Eric: He and Mick had a musical acquaintance from Ealing Club days.

Cooper, Michael: Photographer for classy magazines and who without definite intent brought Marianne and Mick together.

Credland, Judy: She lived in the flat below that of Mick, Keith and Brian in the early days when they lived in Edith Grove, London, W.14. She fed them on many an occasion.

Davies, Cyril: Member of Blues Incorporated who first gave Mick the opportunity of singing before an audience at the Ealing Club.

Doncaster, Patrick: The first British national journalist writing copy on the

Recording artist Marianne Faithfull, uncertain, undecided.

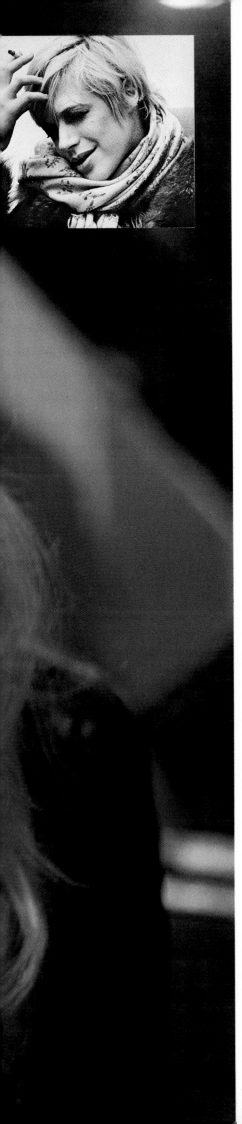

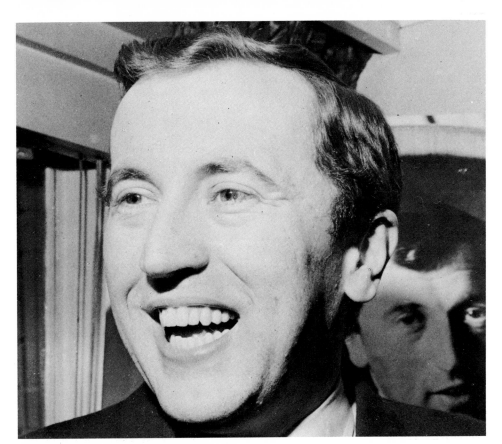

David Frost, who often included the Stones on his T.V. programmes.

Rolling Stones and their music.

Driberg, Tom: A famous British MP who often met and dined with Marianne and Mick when they lived in Marylebone Road and is said to have suggested Mick might try his hand at politics.

Dunbar, John: A Cambridge graduate who married Marianne Faithfull. They had one son, Nicholas.

Dunn, Alan: An Executive of the 1972 Stones tour of America and afterwards of the London office.

Easton, Eric: A show business agent who was told of the amazing scenes created by the Stones at Richmond by writer-journalist, Peter Jones. With Andrew Oldham he went and heard the group and the two became co-managers.

Faithfull, Marianne: Recording artist, stage actress and once girlfriend of Mick Jagger. She was one of the people interviewed by Anthony Scaduto for his book on Mick. The Stones did not talk with the celebrated writer. Mick Jagger said Marianne told many lies about him. Her career during the time when she was involved with the Stones was rent with drama. At one time she lost an expected child which would have been Mick's. She almost took her life and suffered from the effects and withdrawal from heroin.

In 1975 she made new recordings and played a theatre tour of Britain and appeared to be successfully building a new career after some years away from the music business scene.

Firth, Dr Dixon: He appeared for Mick Jagger at his famous drug trial and said he had given oral permission for the singer to use pep pills.

Fox, James: Co-star with Mick Jagger in the film, *Performance*.

Frost, David: Famous British TV personality on whose show Mick Jagger appeared on several occasions. The Stones also played on his show.

Garcia, Jerry: Leader of the group Grateful Dead who suggested to Mick that the Stones should play a free concert at the end of their '69 tour. It was held at Altamont.

Gomelsky, Giorgio: Promoter of the British National Blues and Jazz Conventions and club owner of the Crawdaddy, Station Hotel, Richmond. He hired the Stones as residents.

Graham, Bill: Famous US rock promoter and acted in this capacity many times for the Stones.

Hendrix, Jimi: Admired by Mick Jagger. Mick often went and heard him play at London's Speakeasy Club.

Hopkins, Rev. Hugh: The priest who officiated at the funeral service and the burial of the late Brian Jones.

Hopkins, Nicky: Originally became known through working on The Who's *My Generation* album. He has played on all the Rolling Stones' albums since *Their Satanic Majesties* and played with them on their 1972 American tour. Mick Taylor played with him on his first solo album *The Tin Man Was A Dreamer* (CBS). He has also played with many other famous rock musicians including a period with the Jeff Beck group and recording work with Steve Miller, Jefferson Airplane, John Lennon and George Harrison. He is one of rock's most accomplished keyboard men.

Hunt, Marsha: One-time girlfriend of Mick Jagger and claimed mother of a child resulting from their relationship.

Hunter, Meredith: 18-year-old killed in front of the Stones' stage at Altamont.

Jagger, Chris: Brother of Mick. Has had his own recording contract. Rarely seen in brother's company.

Jagger, Joe, Eva: Father and mother of Mick Jagger. They attended his wedding with Bianca but have steered clear of the limelight.

Jenner, Peter: Director of organization responsible for arranging Hyde Park, London, open-air concerts and with whom Mick Jagger talked concerning the memorable 5 July concert.

Johns, Glyn: Often engineer and sometimes producer of Rolling Stones recorded material.

Jones, Paul: Not the Paul of Manfred Mann and solo career. He sang on stage with Brian Jones at the Ealing Club.

Jones, Peter: The journalist who discovered the Stones and set the ball rolling for their success. Jones was a freelance journalist working for *Record Mirror* and was reporter, features editor and finally editor of the British pop weekly. He now works for the British trade paper, *Music Week,* freelances for countless journals and is author of several books.

Jopling, Norman: *Record Mirror* journalist and first feature copywriter on the Stones.

Keates, Linda: One time girlfriend of Keith Richard.

Kenner, Janice: Once worked for Mick Jagger at his Stargroves home.

Keylock, Tom: Chauffeur to Brian Jones and once the same for Keith Richard. He was at the house when Mick and Marianne came in an effort to re-establish relations with Brian Jones.

Right: The Jagger family at Mick's wedding. Due to the crush, the story says, they had not given their wedding present at the day's end. Inset: Chris Jagger, who has shunned limelight and publicity.

Nicky Hopkins' piano playing added lift and life to the Stones' music, and although he has never been an official Stone, he has often joined them on disc and stage.

Klein, Allen: Once business manager for the Rolling Stones and introduced by the Stones to John Lennon.

Korner, Alexis: Much respected musical figure and a person with considerable musical influence upon many artists. Among his activities was having his Alexis Korner Band resident at London's Marquee Jazz Club. The Stones deputized for his band one evening. Korner was impressed with their work and obtained for them regular work at Ealing and the Marquee clubs. One of his band members was Charlie Watts. When his band played at Cheltenham he was spoken to after the concert by a local person called Brian Jones. Korner gave Brian his London address and telephone number. Korner was influential in the British blues scene of the time and among the musical group he belonged to were the jazz bands of Chris Barber and Ken Colyer.

Lawson, Janet: Nurse to Brian Jones and with him on the night he tragically died.

Lennon, John: A friend of the band and Mick.

Martin, Dean: American show-business personality on whose show the Stones featured in their early days and suffered innumerable caustic comments about their appearance.

McCartney, Paul: With John Lennon gave the Stones the song 'I Wanna Be Your Man'.

McDonald, Carol: Met the Stones in New York and was part of a general British package tour which included Goldie & The Gingerbreads.

Miller, Jimmy: Record producer with the Stones, from 2 March 1967.

Monck, Chip: Lighting expert of many a Stones tour.

Moore, Stan: 'Mr Security' of the 1972 USA tour.

Morris, John: Once in charge of London's rock venue, The Rainbow, a promoter, at one time possible producer of the Stones' 1972 tour.

Left: Alexis Korner, one of the musical inspirations of the Stones in the early years. He encouraged them from the start, and often played with them. Below: The Beatles. They were the only group to achieve greater fame and success than the Stones.

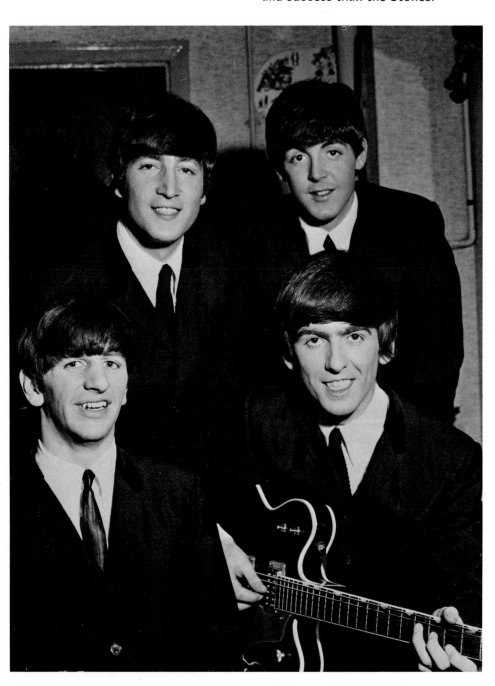

Far left: Allen Klein, famous business manager not only of the Stones but also of the Beatles. John Lennon and Paul McCartney wrote 'I Wanna Be Your Man', an early Stones' hit.

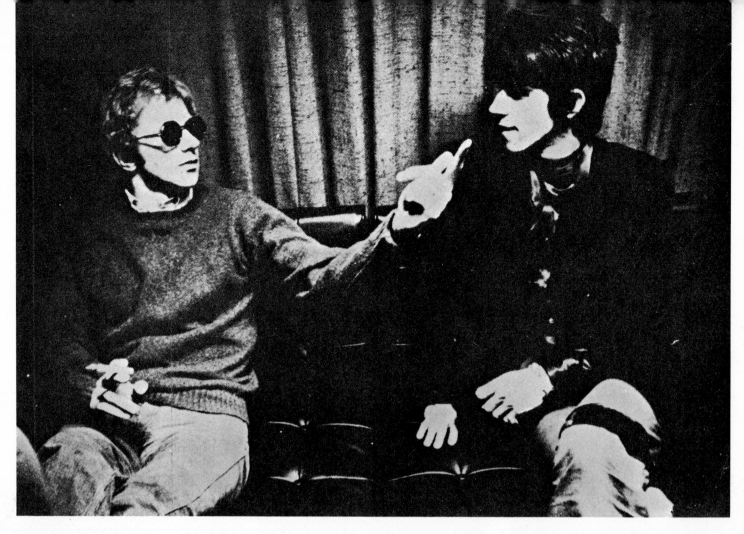

Oldham, Andrew: Andrew Oldham heard the Stones at Richmond on the recommendation of Peter Jones. He was a publicist and aged 19. He and Eric Easton became co-managers and Oldham, record producer of the group. Oldham later managed and recorded with great success Marianne Faithfull and formed his own record label, Immediate Records. He ceased co-managing the Stones in 1964, though he carried on with recording the group.

Pallenberg, Anita: Once Brian Jones's girlfriend, she later became Keith Richard's. The two are now married and have children.

Parkinson, Dale: One-time solicitor for Mick Jagger and famous for his statement in court which contained the words, 'The Duke of Marlborough had much longer hair than my client and he won some famous battles. His hair was powdered, I think because of fleas and my client has no fleas.'·

Pendleton, Harold: Manager of the Marquee Jazz Club at which the Stones played.

Perrin, Les: Long-valued British publicist of the Stones and has accompanied the Stones on many overseas visits.

Poiter, Suki: One-time girlfriend of Brian Jones.

Above: Andrew Loog Oldham talks with Keith Richard. Below: Keith seen walking with Anita. Right: Brian enjoys a joke with Andrew.

Above: Mick spotted with Chrissie Shrimpton, sister of world famous model Jean. Chrissie was Mick's girlfriend for some time, but was succeeded by Marianne Faithfull in Mick's affections. Right: Phil Spector pondering another hit.

Proby, P. J.: He became boyfriend of Chrissie Shrimpton for a time after she had walked out on boyfriend, Mick Jagger.

Radziwill, Princess Lee: One of many wealthy people who accompanied the Stones during much of their 1972 tour. She is part of the Kennedy family.

Rees Mogg, William: Editor of the London *Times* and responsible for the famous editorial attacking the process of British justice concerning sentences imposed upon Mick Jagger and Keith Richard.

Ricci: London hairdresser famous for attention to Mrs Bianca Jagger's hair.

Richardson, Tony: Producer of the film, *Ned Kelly*, in which Mick played the role of the hero, Ned.

Rowe, Dick: An official of Decca record company who signed the Stones.

Rudge, Peter: Promoter. Co-producer of the 1972 American tour.

Sandison, David: Les Perrin's deputy who handled publicity on the 1972 tour.

Schifano, Mario: Marianne Faithfull lived with him for a time after leaving Mick Jagger.

Schneider, Ronnie: Nephew of Allen Klein and hired to produce the 1972 tour.

Schreiderma, Henry: Mysterious American or Canadian person at Keith Richard's house when raided by the police.

Shrimpton, Chrissie: Sister of famous model, Jean. She lived with Mick almost from the group's first footing in the record world until their parting, at which time Mick had turned towards Marianne Faithfull. She once left Mick for P. J. Proby.

Spector, Phil: Famous US producer who worked briefly with the Stones in their early days as a co-writer and producer with Mick of a B side.

Sullivan, Ed: Legendary US television music show presenter. The Stones' appearances on his show were always punctuated by previous conflict.

Sylvester, Cleo: Mick once asked her in the band's early days whether she, with several other girls, could provide some girl vocal backing and thus attempt something akin to American recordings.

Taylor, Dick: Classmate with Mick at Dartford Grammar School and a member of a teen group which Mick joined called Little Boy Blue and the Blue Boys. He attended Sidcup Art School and there met Keith Richard. For a time he kept with them but then dropped out. He did offer someone like Keith considerable encouragement. He later helped form The Pretty Things.

Thurogood, Frank: A building contractor and at Brian Jones's house at the time the singer died.

Whitehouse, Mary: Chairman of the British Viewers and Listeners Association, a self-appointed body, who once debated with Mick Jagger about his views on a major British TV show.

Wohlin, Anna: One-time girlfriend of Brian Jones and with him on the night of his death.

DISCOGRAPHY

Photo Dick Burrows.

531/10 ↓ ↑ 531/9 531/12 ↓ ↑ 531/11

EPS:

The Rolling Stones January 1964
'Bye Bye Johnny'; 'Money'; 'You Better Move On'; 'Poison Ivy'

Five by Five August 1964
'If You Need Me'; 'Empty Heart'; 'Confessin' The Blues'; 'Around And Around'

Got Live If You Want It June 1965
'We Want The Stones'; 'Everybody Needs Somebody To Love'; 'Pain In My Heart'; 'Route 66'; 'I'm Moving On'; 'I'm Alright'

Street Fighting Man June 1972
'Street Fighting Man'; 'Surprise, Surprise'; 'Everybody Needs Somebody To Love'

ALBUMS:

The Rolling Stones April 1964
'Route 66'; 'I Just Want To Make Love To You'; 'Honest I Do'; 'I Need You Baby'; 'Now I've Got A Witness'; 'Little By Little'; 'I'm A King Bee'; 'Carol'; 'Tell Me'; 'Can I Get A Witness'; 'You Can Make It If You Try'; 'Walking The Dog'.

The Rolling Stones No. 2 January 1965
'Everybody Needs Somebody To Love'; 'Down Home Girl'; 'You Can't Catch Me'; 'Time Is On My Side'; 'What A Shame'; 'Grown Up Wrong'; 'Down The Road Apiece'; 'Under The Boardwalk'; 'I Can't Be Satisfied'; 'Pain In My Heart'; 'Off The Hook'; 'Susie-Q'.

With others: Lord's Taverners May 1965

Out Of Our Heads September 1965
'She Said Yeah'; 'Mercy, Mercy'; 'Hitch Hike'; 'That's How Strong My Love Is'; 'Good Times'; 'Gotta Get Away'; 'Talkin' 'Bout You'; 'Cry To Me'; 'Oh Baby (We Got A Good Thing Going)'; 'Heart Of Stone'; 'The Under Assistant West Coast Promotion Man'; 'I'm Free'.

Aftermath April 1966
'Mother's Little Helper'; 'Stupid Girl'; 'Lady Jane'; 'Under My Thumb'; 'Doncha Bother Me'; 'Goin' Home'; 'Flight 505'; 'High And Dry'; 'Out Of Time'; 'It's Not Easy'; 'I Am Waiting'; 'Take It Or Leave It'; 'Think'; 'What To Do'.

RELEASED ON DECCA (UK)

SINGLES

		highest chart position
'Come On'	June 1963	21
'I Wanna Be Your Man'	November 1963	12
'Not Fade Away'	February 1964	3
'It's All Over Now'	July 1964	1
'Little Red Rooster'	November 1964	1
'The Last Time'	February 1965	1
'(I Can't Get No) Satisfaction'	August 1965	1
'Get Off Of My Cloud'	October 1965	1
'19th Nervous Breakdown'	February 1966	2
'Paint It Black'	May 1966	1
'Have You Seen Your Mother, Baby'	September 1966	5
'Let's Spend The Night Together'/'Ruby Tuesday'	January 1967	8
'We Love You'/'Dandelion'	August 1967	8
'Jumpin' Jack Flash'	May 1968	1
'Honky Tonk Women'	July 1969	1
'Street Fighting Man'	July 1971	—
'Sad Day'	May 1973	—
'Don't Know Why'	May 1975	—
'Out Of Time'	September 1975	45

Solo single:
Mick Jagger 'Memo To Turner'	November 1970	

Early recording sessions often lasted for days. The group found problems in re-creating their stage excitement in a recording studio, away from the cheering crowds.

Big Hits (High Tide And Green Grass) November 1966
'Have You Seen Your Mother, Baby'; 'Paint It Black'; 'It's All Over Now'; 'The Last Time'; 'Heart Of Stone'; 'Not Fade Away'; 'Come On'; '(I Can't Get No) Satisfaction'; 'Get Off Of My Cloud'; 'As Tears Go By'; '19th Nervous Breakdown'; 'Lady Jane'; 'Time Is On My Side'; 'Little Red Rooster'.

Between The Buttons January 1967
'Yesterday's Papers'; 'My Obsession'; 'Back Street Girl'; 'Connection'; 'She Smiled Sweetly'; 'Cool, Calm And Collected'; 'All Sold Out'; 'Please Go Home'; 'Who's Been Sleeping Here?'; 'Complicated'; 'Miss Amanda Jones'; 'Something Happened To Me Yesterday'.

Their Satanic Majesties December 1967
'Sing This All Together'; 'Citadel'; 'In Another Land'; '2,000 Man'; 'Sing This Altogether (See What Happens)'; 'She's A Rainbow'; 'The Lattern'; 'Gomper'; '2,000 Light Years From Home'; 'On With The Show'.

Beggars Banquet December 1968
'Sympathy For The Devil'; 'No Expectations'; 'Dear Doctor'; 'Parachute Woman'; 'Jig-Saw Puzzle'; 'Street Fighting Man'; 'Prodigal Son'; 'Stray Cat Blues'; 'Factory Girl'; 'Salt Of The Earth'.

Through The Past Darkly (Big Hits, Vol. 2) September 1969
'Jumpin' Jack Flash'; 'Mother's Little Helper'; '2,000 Light Years From Home'; 'Let's Spend The Night Together'; 'You Better Move On'; 'We Love You'; 'Street Fighting Man'; 'She's A Rainbow'; 'Ruby Tuesday' 'Dandelion'; 'Sittin' On A Fence'; 'Honky Tonk Women'.

Let It Bleed January 1970
'Gimme Shelter'; 'Love In Vain'; 'Country Honk'; 'Live With Me'; 'Let It Bleed'; 'Midnight Rambler'; 'You Got The Silver'; 'Monkey Man'; 'You Can't Always Get What You Want'.

Get Yer Ya-Yas Out September 1970
'Jumpin' Jack Flash'; 'Carol'; 'Stray Cat Blues'; 'Love In Vain'; 'Midnight Rambler'; 'Sympathy For The Devil'; 'Live With Me'; 'Little Queenie'; 'Honky Tonk Women'; 'Street Fighting Man'.

Stone Age March 1971
'Look What You've Done'; 'It's All Over Now'; 'Confessin' The Blues'; 'One More Try'; 'As Tears Go By'; 'The Spider And The Fly'; 'My Girl'; 'Paint It Black'; 'If You Need Me'; 'The Last Time'; 'Blue Turns To Grey'; 'Around And Around'.

Gimme Shelter August 1971
'Jumpin' Jack Flash'; 'Love In Vain'; 'Honky Tonk Women'; 'Street Fighting Man'; 'Sympathy For The Devil'; 'Gimme Shelter'; 'Under My Thumb'; 'I've Been Loving You Too Long';

'Fortune Teller'; 'Lady Jane'; '(I Can't Get No) Satisfaction'.

Milestones February 1972
'Satisfaction'; 'She's A Rainbow'; 'Under My Thumb'; 'I Just Wanna Make Love To You'; 'Yesterday's Papers'; 'I Wanna Be Your Man'; 'Time Is On My Side'; 'Get Off Of My Cloud'; 'Not Fade Away'; 'Out Of Time'; 'She Said Yeah'; 'Stray Cat Blues'.

Rock 'n' Rolling Stones October 1972
'Route 66'; 'The Under Assistant West Coast Promotion Man'; 'Come On'; 'Talkin' 'Bout You'; 'Bye Bye Johnny'; 'Down The Road'; 'I Just Wanna Make Love To You'; 'Everybody Needs Somebody To Love'; 'Oh Baby (We Got A Good Thing Going)'; '19th Nervous Breakdown'; 'Little Queenie'; 'Carol'.

No Stone Unturned October 1973
'Poison Ivy'; 'The Singer Not The Song'; 'Surprise, Surprise'; 'Child Of The Moon'; 'Stoned'; 'Sad Day'; 'Money'; 'Congratulations'; 'I'm Movin' On'; '2120 South Michigan Avenue'; 'Long Long While'; 'Who's Driving Your Plane?'.

Metamorphosis July 1975
'Out Of Time'; 'Don't Lie To Me'; 'Some Things Just Stick In Your Mind'; 'Each And Everyday Of The Year'; 'Heart Of Stone'; 'I'd Rather Be With The Boys'; '(Walkin' Thru The) Sleepy City'; 'We're Wastin' Time'; 'Try A Little Harder'; 'I Don't Know Why'; 'If You Let Me'; 'Jiving Sister Fanny'; 'Downtown Suzie'; 'Family'; 'Memo to Turner'; 'I'm Going Down'.

Rolled Gold November 1975
(The Very Best Of The Rolling Stones): 'Come On'; 'I Wanna Be Your Man'; 'Not Fade Away'; 'Carol'; 'It's All Over Now'; 'Little Red Rooster'; 'Time Is On My Side'; 'The Last Time'; '(I Can't Get No) Satisfaction'; 'Get Off Of My Cloud'; '19th Nervous Breakdown'; 'As Tears Go By'; 'Under My Thumb'; 'Lady Jane'; 'Out Of Time'; 'Paint It Black'; 'Have You Seen Your Mother, Baby'; 'Let's Spend The Night Together'; 'Ruby Tuesday'; 'Yesterday's Papers'; 'We Love You'; 'She's A Rainbow'; 'Jumpin' Jack Flash'; 'Honky Tonk Women'; 'Sympathy For The Devil'; 'Street Fighting Man'; 'Midnight Rambler'; 'Gimme Shelter'.

COMMENTS: This list is Rolling Stones material as issued by the Decca Record Company. The two parted company and the first Rolling Stones material on Rolling Stones Records was a single issued on 23 April 1971. As the list makes plain, Decca have continued releasing material, made available to them under their contract,

previous to 1971. Thus all material from that date is not new recording.

RELEASED ON ROLLING STONES RECORDS (UK).

SINGLES:

'Brown Sugar'	April 1971
'Tumblin' Dice'	April 1972
'Angie'	August 1973

'Brown Sugar' (re-issued on 208 Atlantic Gold Series) January 1974. 'It's Only Rock 'n' Roll' July 1974.

ALBUMS:

Sticky Fingers April 1971
'Brown Sugar'; 'Sway'; 'Wild Horses'; 'Can't You Hear Me Knocking'; 'You Gotta Move'; 'Bitch'; 'I Got The Blues'; 'Sister Morphine'; 'Dead Flowers'; 'Moonlight Mile'.

Exile On Main Street May 1972
'Rocks Off'; 'Rip This Joint'; 'Shake Your Hips'; 'Casino Boogie'; 'Tumblin' Dice'; 'Sweet Virginia'; 'Torn And Frayed'; 'Sweet Black Angel'; 'Loving Cup'; 'Happy'; 'Turd On The Run'; 'Ventilator Blues'; 'I Just Want To See His Face'; 'Let It Loose'; 'All Down The Line'; 'Stop Breaking Down'; 'Shine A Light'; 'Soul Survivor'.

Goat's Head Soup August 1973
'Dancing With Mr D'; '100 Years Ago'; 'Coming Down Again'; 'Doo Doo Doo Doo Doo (Heartbreaker)'; 'Angie'; 'Silver Train'; 'Hide Your Love'; 'Winter'; 'Can You Hear The Music'; 'Star, Star'.

It's Only Rock 'n' Roll October 1974
'If You Can't Rock Me'; 'Ain't Too Proud To Beg'; 'It's Only Rock 'n' Roll'; 'Till The Next Goodbye'; 'Time Waits For No-One'; 'Luxury'; 'Dance Little Sister'; 'If You Really Want To By My Friend'; 'Short And Curlies'; 'Fingerprint File'.

Made In The Shade June 1975
'Brown Sugar'; 'Tumblin' Dice'; 'Happy'; 'Dance Little Sister'; 'Wild Horses'; 'Angie'; 'Bitch'; 'It's Only Rock 'n' Roll'; 'Doo Doo Doo Doo Doo (Heartbreaker)'; 'Rip This Joint'; 'Luxury'; 'Ain't Too Proud To Beg'; 'Fingerprint File'; 'If You Can't Rock Me'.

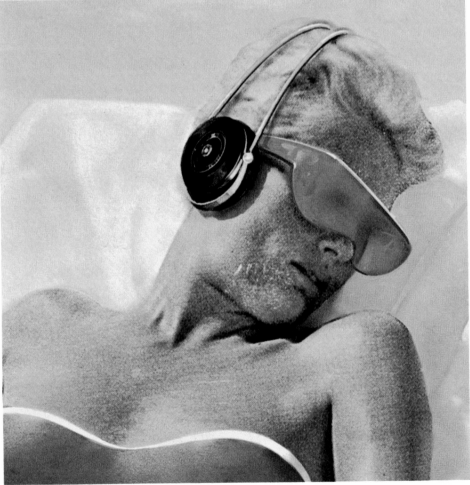

OTHER ALBUMS

The London Howlin' Wolf Sessions
November 1971
Bill Wyman, bass, shakers, cowbell; Ian Stewart, piano; Charlie Watts, drums, conga, asstd. percussion.

Jamming With Edward January 1972
The album featured Nicky Hopkins, Ry Cooder, Mick Jagger, Bill Wyman and Charlie Watts.

BILL WYMAN: SINGLES

'White Lightnin'/'Monkey Grip Glue' November 1975

ALBUM:

Monkey Grip May 1974
'I Wanna Get Me A Gun'; 'Crazy Woman'; 'Pussy'; 'Mighty Fine Time'; 'Monkey Grip Glue'; 'What A Blow'; 'White Lightnin''; 'I'll Pull You Through'; 'It's A Wonder'.

THE STONES IN AMERICA

Singles:

title	year	highest chart position (as recorded by *Billboard*)
'Not Fade Away'	1964	48
'Tell Me'	1964	24
'It's All Over Now'	1964	26
'Time Is On My Side'	1964	6
'Heart Of Stone'	1965	19
'The Last Time'	1965	9
'Play With Fire'	1965	96
'(I Can't Get No) Satisfaction'	1965	1
'Get Off Of My Cloud'	1965	1
'As Tears Go By'	1965	6
'19th Nervous Breakdown'	1966	2
'Paint It Black'	1966	1
'Have You Seen Your Mother, Baby'	1966	9
'Mother's Little Helper'	1966	8
'Let's Spend The Night Together'	1967	55
'Ruby Tuesday'	1967	1
'We Love You'/'Dandelion'	1967	50
'She's A Rainbow'/'2,000 Light Years'	1967	25
'Jumpin' Jack Flash'	1968	3
'Street Fighting Man'	1968	48
'Honky Tonk Women'	1969	1
'Brown Sugar'	1971	1
'Wild Horses'	1971	—
'Tumblin' Dice'	1972	7
'Happy'	1972	22
'Angie'	1973	1
'Doo Doo Doo Doo Doo (Heartbreaker)'	1973	—
'It's Only Rock 'n' Roll'	1974	16
'Ain't Too Proud'	1974	17

ROLLING STONES material available in the States

Obviously there is similarity in material which is released in the US, but particularly in the early days content was tracked differently from the UK listing and sometimes, switched from one album to another.

ALBUMS:

The Rolling Stones' First Album:
'Not Fade Away'; 'Route 66'; 'I Just Want To Make Love To You'; 'Honest I Do'; 'Now I've Got A Witness'; 'Little By Little'; 'I'm A King Bee'; 'Carol'; 'Tell Me'; 'Can I Get A Witness'; 'You Can Make It If You Try'; 'Walking The Dog'.

12 By 5
'Around And Around'; 'Confessin' The Blues'; 'Empty Heart'; 'Time Is On My Side'; 'Good Times Bad Times'; 'It's All Over Now'; '2120 South Michigan Avenue'; 'Under The Boardwalk'; 'Congratulations'; 'Grown Up Wrong'; 'If You Need Me'; 'Susie-Q'.

Rolling Stones, Now!
'Everybody Needs Somebody To Love'; 'Down Home Girl'; 'You Can't Catch Me'; 'Heart Of Stone'; 'What A Shame'; 'I Need You Baby'; 'Down The Road Apiece'; 'Off The Hook'; 'Pain In My Heart'; 'Oh, Baby (We Got A Good Thing Going)'; 'Little Red Rooster'; 'Surprise, Surprise'.

Out Of Our Heads
'Mercy Mercy'; 'Hitch Hike'; 'The Last Time'; 'That's How Strong My Love Is'; 'Good Times'; 'I'm Alright'; '(I Can't Get No) Satisfaction'; 'Cry To Me'; 'The Under Assistant West Coast Promotion Man'; 'Play With Fire'; 'The Spider And The Fly'; 'One More Try'.

December's Children (And Everybody's)
'She Said Yeah'; 'Talkin' 'Bout You'; 'You Better Move On'; 'Look What You've Done'; 'The Singer Not The Song'; 'Route 66'; 'Get Off Of My Cloud'; 'I'm Free'; 'As Tears Go By'; 'Gotta Get Away'; 'Blue Turns To Grey'; 'I'm Movin' On'.

Aftermath
As for the UK though with different track order and the omission of 'Out Of Time'; 'Take It Or Leave It'.

Got Live If You Want It!
'Under My Thumb'; 'Get Off Of My Cloud'; 'Lady Jane'; 'Not Fade Away'; 'I've Been Loving You Too Long'; 'Fortune Teller'; 'The Last Time'; '19th Nervous Breakdown'; 'Time Is On My Side'; 'I'm Alright'; 'Have You Seen Your Mother, Baby'; '(I Can't Get No) Satisfaction'.

Between The Buttons
As for the UK save for the addition of 'Let's Spend The Night Together' and deletion of 'Please Go Home' and 'Back Street Girl'.

Flowers
'Ruby Tuesday'; 'Have You Seen Your Mother, Baby'; 'Let's Spend The Night Together'; 'Lady Jane'; 'Out Of Time'; 'My Girl'; 'Backstreet Girl'; 'Please Go Home'; 'Mother's Little Helper'; 'Take It Or Leave It'; 'Ride On Baby'; 'Sittin' On A Fence'.

Big Hits (High Tide And Green Grass)
'19th Nervous Breakdown'; '(I Can't Get No) Satisfaction'; 'Tell Me'; 'Get Off Of My Cloud'; 'As Tears Go By'; 'Heart Of Stone'; 'Play With Fire'; 'Time Is On My Side'; 'It's All Over Now'; 'Not Fade Away'; 'The Last Time'; 'Good Times, Bad Times'.

Their Satanic Majesties Request
As the UK track listing.

Beggars Banquet
As for the UK release.

Through The Past Darkly (Big Hits, Vol. 2)
'Honky Tonk Women'; 'Ruby Tuesday'; 'Jumpin' Jack Flash'; 'Street Fighting Man'; 'Let's Spend The Night Together'; '2,000 Light Years From Home'; 'Mother's Little Helper'; 'Sittin' On A Fence'; 'You Better Move On'; 'She's A Rainbow'; 'We Love You'; 'Dandelion'.

Let It Bleed
'Let It Bleed'; 'Love In Vain'; 'Midnight Rambler'; 'Gimme Shelter'; 'You Got The Silver'; 'You Can't Always Get What You Want'; 'Live With Me'; 'Monkey Man'; 'Country Honk'.

Hot Rocks (double-record set)
'Time Is On My Side'; 'Heart Of Stone'; 'Play With Fire'; '(I Can't Get No) Satisfaction'; 'As Tears Go By'; 'Get Off Of My Cloud'; 'Mother's Little Helper'; '19th Nervous Breakdown'; 'Paint It Black'; 'Under My Thumb'; 'Ruby Tuesday'; 'Let's Spend The Night Together'; 'Jumpin' Jack Flash'; 'Street Fighting Man'; 'Sympathy For The Devil'; 'Honky Tonk Women'; 'Gimme Shelter'; 'Midnight Rambler' (live); 'You Can't Always Get What You Want'; 'Brown Sugar'; 'Wild Horses'.

Get Yer Ya-Yas Out
'Jumpin' Jack Flash'; 'Carol'; 'Stray Cat Blues'; 'Love In Vain'; 'Midnight Rambler'; 'Sympathy For The Devil'; 'Live With Me'; 'Little Queenie'; 'Honky Tonk Women'; 'Street Fighting Man'.

More Hot Rocks (Big Hits & Fazed Cookies)
'Tell Me'; 'Not Fade Away'; 'Last Time'; 'It's All Over Now'; 'Good Times, Bad Times'; 'I'm Free'; 'Out Of Time'; 'Lady Jane'; 'Sittin' On A Fence'; 'Have You Seen Your Mother, Baby'; 'Dandelion'; 'We Love You'; 'She's A Rainbow'; '2,000 Light Years From Home'; 'Child Of The Moon'; 'No Expectations'; 'Let It Bleed'; 'What To Do'; 'Money'; 'Fortune Teller'; 'Poison Ivy'; 'Bye Bye Johnny'; 'I Can't Be Satisfied'; 'Long, Long While'.

Metamorphosis

'Ana'; 'Out Of Time'; 'Don't Lie To Me'; 'Each And Every Day Of The Year'; 'Heart Of Stone'; 'I'd Much Rather Be With The Boys'; '(Walkin' Thru The) Sleepy City'; 'Try A Little Harder'; 'I Don't Know Why'; 'If You Let Me'; 'Jiving Sister Fannie'; 'Downtown Suzie'; 'Family'; 'Memo To Turner'; 'I'm Going Down'.

AS FOR THE UK:
Exile On Main Street

Made In The Shade

Sticky Fingers

Goat's Head Soup

It's Only Rock 'n' Roll

IN AMERICA ONLY:
Re-packaging as a double album release: **Stone Age/Got Live**

ROLLING STONES: Releases worldwide. On Rolling Stones Records and date of release.

SINGLES:

'Brown Sugar'/'Bitch'; Australia 5/71; Japan 4/71; New Zealand 5/71; Argentina 8/71; Brazil 5/71; Hong Kong 6/71; Mexico 5/71; Peru 6/71; Venezuela 5/71.
'Wild Horses'/'Sway': Australia 7/71; Japan 8/71; New Zealand 7/71; South Africa 7/71; Hong Kong 8/71; Mexico 9/71; Venezuela 8/71.
'Tumblin' Dice'/'Sweet Black Angel': Japan 5/71; Argentina 6/71; Brazil 6/72; El Salvador 6/72; Hong Kong 4/72; Philippines 6/72; Venezuela 4/72.
'Happy'/'All Down The Line': Japan 9/72; Brazil 11/72; Philippines 9/72.
'Angie'/'Silver Train': Canada 8/73; Japan 9/73; Argentina 12/73; Brazil 4/74; El Salvador 2/74; Lebanon 2/73; Peru 12/73; Uruguay 2/74; Zambia 12/73.

'Doo Doo Doo Doo Doo (Heartbreaker)'/'Dancing With Mr D': Canada 1/74; Japan 3/74; New Zealand 12/73; Brazil 4/74; India 7/74; Turkey 12/74.
'It's Only Rock 'n' Roll'/'Through The Lonely Nights': Australia 9/74; Canada 7/74; Japan 9/74; New Zealand 8/74; Argentina 11/74; El Salvador 9/74; India 1/75; Singapore 9/74; Turkey 12/74; Uruguay 9/74; Venezuela 8/74.
'Ain't Too Proud'/'Dance Little Sister': Australia 1/75; Canada 11/74; Japan 2/75; New Zealand 1/75; Brazil 2/75.

BILL WYMAN

'I Wanna Get Me A Gun'/'White Lightnin': Canada 7/74; New Zealand 5/74.
'Monkey Grip Glue'/'White Lightnin': Australia 8/74; New Zealand 7/74.

ALBUMS:

Exile On Main Street: Australia 7/72; New Zealand 8/72; Argentina 8/72; Brazil 9/72; Chile 5/72; Mexico

8/72; Philippines 1/73; Uruguay 3/74; Venezuela 6/72.

Sticky Fingers: Australia 7/71; Canada 5/71; Japan 5/71; New Zealand 10/71; South Africa 1/71; Argentina 8/71; Brazil 7/71; Colombia 6/71; Ecuador 9/71; Hong Kong 6/71; Israel 4/72; Mexico 5/71; Philippines 9/71; Venezuela 6/71.

Goat's Head Soup: Japan 10/73; New Zealand 9/74; Argentina 11/73; Colombia 11/73; India 6/74; Israel

2/72; Lebanon 10/73; Philippines 5/74; Uruguay 1/74; West Indies 11/73.

It's Only Rock 'n' Roll: Australia 10/74; Canada 10/74; Japan 10/74; New Zealand 10/74; Brazil 12/74; Colombia 9/74; El Salvador 1/75; India 3/75; Israel 2/74; Lebanon 11/74; Mexico 3/75; Uruguay 2/75; Venezuela 9/74.

Made In The Shade: Canada 6/75; South Africa 6/75; Hong Kong 6/75.

OTHER ALBUMS:
Jamming With Edwards: Australia 4/72; Canada 2/72; Japan 3/72; New Zealand 4/72; Brazil 2/72; Hong Kong 4/72; Mexico 2/72; Philippines 12/73; Venezuela 4/72.

Brian Jones Presents The Pipes Of Pan At Jau Jauka: Australia 1/72; Canada 11/71; Japan 12/71; Hong Kong 12/71.

The London Howlin' Wolf Sessions* Japan 10/71; New Zealand 12/71; South Africa 2/72; Hong Kong 4/72; Mexico 3/72.
Monkey Grip (Bill Wyman): Australia 7/74; Canada 5/74; Japan 7/74; New Zealand 7/74; Hong Kong 5/74; Israel 10/74; Lebanon 10/74.

All discs also issued in the United States.

*Howlin' Wolf whose real name is Chester Burnett died on Saturday, 10 January 1976. He supplied classic Stones songs, 'Little Red Rooster' and 'Spoonful'. They heard his original and liked it. His *London Sessions* album on Rolling Stones records in 1971 was his last major recording. As noted elsewhere, several of the Stones took part in the sessions, as did Stevie Wonder and Eric Clapton.

The Rolling Stones have also appeared on two LPs—recording of a BBC Radio programme, Saturday Club and Ready Steady Go!, an Independent Television show.

On 15 November 1969, the British music paper *Record Mirror* announced 'Stones LP You Can't Buy'. This was an LP simply titled *The Rolling Stones* and given a pressing of 200 copies and made for radio presentation/ promotion for disc jockeys and show producers. The album featured: 'Route 66'; 'Walking The Dog'; 'Around And Around'; 'Everybody Needs Somebody'; 'Susie-Q'; 'I'm Free'; 'She Said Yeah'; 'Under My Thumb'; 'Stupid Girl'; '2,000'; 'Sympathy For The Devil'; 'Prodigal Son' and 'Love In Vain'.

This writer does not doubt that the Stones are the greatest live band in rock history. Other people may have produced better records or given more memorable stage performances but they have lacked consistency and staying power or, as in the case of the Beatles, have become studio based. One arguable exception is The Who.

The Stones have had their uneven moments without anywhere near touching rock bottom. They have maintained themselves as a top-rated band now for more than thirteen years. And apart from the tragic death of Brian Jones, their basic line-up has remained constant with Bill Wyman, Charlie Watts, Keith Richard and Mick Jagger.

They have even broken the law of rock music, that no one comes back more powerful a second time. The Stones have had several lengthy interruptions in their career and bounced back bigger than before and carrying with them a new generation or two.

In Mick Jagger they have rock's finest live performer and vocalist and indeed via him the Stones have often been well ahead of the rock scene itself. Long before people used the term 'theatre rock', the Stones were up to their tricks. Jagger was involved with stories of bisexuality, into camp, utilizing make-up, acting the decadent, well before David Bowie and others of similar ilk made it fashionable.

Whether the Stones have influenced youth and whether they have caused or helped to cause moral degradation are speculative questions. The first is perhaps easier to answer than the second: they have sold millions of records and performed before millions of people, and since most people do not pay out money for records or concerts without reason, one assumes it is because what the Stones do, say and play makes sense. The Stones may be more than mere entertainment; they may act out in their world of music just what some of the fans feel or would like to find in their world. The Stones may present pictures of life which the fans feel correspond with reality. They will only be brief pictures since a show or an album can only depict a few aspects.

Certainly the Stones have expressed in their music and sometimes in their actions beyond the sphere of show or record, many of society's present ideas and the views held by some contemporary youth. Thus they have emphasized permissiveness, the feeling that traditional society is rotten at its core, 'take it or leave it' personal relations, a love for the satanic, and the desire of many that life should be

as they want it to be and should be lived on their terms.

Whether the Stones caught the spirit of the times, and the ideas were already there below the surface waiting for someone to popularize them, or whether they deliberately started a trend is again debatable. I believe they felt strongly much of what they expressed in those early days in common with large groups of young people their age. Their popularity and consequent attention of the media put them in a situation where their ideas and views then became educative for many people. During the second half of the '60s it suddenly became fashionable for TV and newspaper outlets to interview certain pop figures on a variety of subjects. Pop stars became elevated and they could pontificate. The favourite talkers at the time were Marianne Faithfull, Paul Jones and Mick Jagger.

The Stones became leaders whether they wished it or not. Their music became personal and social anthems for many people. However they did not advocate positive life-styles. For most of the time their message is cheerless. They offer no words of salvation, few crumbs of comfort. Fortunately for them, they can enjoy materialistic comforts which still exist in the inflationary West. Their fans may not be so lucky.

Mick Jagger has maintained on several occasions that he, the pop star, cannot be responsible for what the fans may or may not do. He would claim a private life, yet, though the star deserves freedom from much of the publicity nonsense, it seems a trifle self-centred to claim such immunity.

Any objective observer at a Stones or major group concert soon senses that fan-following can know no bounds and for many what a star does and says represents 'style'. The star may not want this but he cannot be unaware that it happens. Can he say, I may choose this way of life, dress in this manner, take drugs, but you must not imitate me. He may ask the fan to think things through for himself, though few stars have said as much.

And it can be argued that many fans have immersed themselves in the more questionable activities which have been part and parcel of some Stones practice. However this lies in the world of speculation. What can be said on the question as to whether the Stones have been a bad moral influence is that they have given prominence to some aspects of living which are not found life-enhancing by groups of people with religious commitment, whether overtly Christian or humanist.

However, is the impact of the Stones any different from that of a documentary or film which highlights certain less savoury aspects of life? One obvious difference surely exists and it brings one back to the star and his responsibility: the Stones have always been associated as people with what they have mirrored in lyric and sound.

Much of their music and some of their style speaks decadence. Some of us would wish it could also offer celebration but whether one has the right to ask this is highly questionable.

Whatever the moral questions may be the Stones are still rock's greatest.

The publishers would like to thank the following individuals and organizations for their kind permission to reproduce the photographs in this book:
Cyrus Andrews: 10–11, 32 left, 45 centre left, 50–51 below, 61 below, 68, 78 above, 84; Associated Press: 24 above, 44 centre, 62 below; Associated Newspapers: 24 below right, 62 below; Black Star: 78 below, 90–91; Clive Bubley: 14–15, 56; Camera Press: 38 below left, 42–43, 54–55; CBS: 74 left; Decca Records: 21 below, 88 left, 89 right; Ian A. Dickson: 73 above left; Globe Photos: 22–23, 92; Peter Jones: 12 left; Keystone Press Agency: 44 above left, 47 below, 52, 57 below, 78–79; London Features International: 28, 46, 63 below, 64 left; David Magnus: 16–17 below centre, 39 below; Octopus Books Ltd: 66–67, 82–83; Photo Features International: 47 above, 48–49 and back end-papers; Pictorial Press: 86 above, 88–89; Popperfoto: 11 below, 16–17 above centre, 18–19, 20 below, 21 above, 25, 30–31, 32–33, 33 below right, 38 below right, 50–51 above, 58–59, 73 right, 76 left; Rex Features: 12–13 above, 13 below, 34–35, 36–37, 40–41, 57 above, 60 below, 62 above, 64–65, 72–73, 76–77, 79, 80–81; Rolling Stones Records: 28–29 above, 86 below left; Showbiz Photo Collection: 8–9; Bill Smith: 53; Syndication International: 16–17 centre, 20 above, 23 above, 26–27, 38–39 above, 44 below right, 45 above right, 45 below right, 55 inset, 58 left, 61 above, 74 right, 80; Chris Walter: 60–61, 63 above, 70–71; Valerie Wilmer: 13 right, 17, 77 right; Wirephoto: 40 left.